"Marvin Olasky has been one of the ~~leading biblically minded jo~~
in America for years. He has shaped *World* magazine's timely and trenchant critique of newsworthy events impacting the American stage of politics, culture and ethics. This selection of his classic articles gives insight, stirs action and prompts reflection as we as believers endeavor to engage our communities with a conscious and consistent Christian worldview."

  Peter A. Lillback, President of Westminster Theological Seminary, Philadelphia, PA

"Interesting, insightful, provocative, remarkably well-informed, and relentlessly biblical in approach, Marvin Olasky's columns are always worth reading, and this book is a rich treasure trove of them. His thoughtful Christian worldview fills this book with a wise analysis of dozens of current issues."

  Wayne Grudem, Research Professor of Theology and Biblical Studies, Phoenix Seminary, Scottsdale, AZ

"Sorting out the urgent from the important is a tough task for everyone, but for Christian believers, it's also sorting out the holy from the hype. Rarely is any issue *the* issue, but it's ONE of many that people of faith must process and confront. In his new book, Marvin Olasky provides a rational and thoughtful process to prevent us from 'using *all* our water for too small a fire' as my college professor used to remind me. Dealing with same-sex 'marriage,' abortion, bathroom laws, faith-hating films, court decisions, and political conflicts are just a few of the issues we face. But no one issue should consume us. Christ should consume us. Olasky's approach is like Nexium to the indigestion of the soul."

  Mike Huckabee, Former governor of Arkansas

"America may be more culturally and politically divided today than at any time since the Civil War. Christians need to know how to act and live smartly and prudently, with strength and compassion. Employing his usual wisdom and clarity, Marvin Olasky explains how."

  William J. Bennett, Former US Secretary of Education; host of the *Bill Bennett Show*

"*World View: Seeking Grace and Truth in Our Common Life* offers practical theology without hysterics, histrionics, or sell-outs. This wise book, written by a sage veteran of cultural shifts and values, models how to live like a Christian in a world losing its foundations. As editor of *World* magazine, Marvin Olasky, with both street cred and old-school professional authority, illustrates by example what civil discourse means and how we must practice it. Practical, readable, accessible, transparent, and relevant to all. Olasky blazes a trail for those who want to talk with their neighbors, not blast them on social media. He speaks to those of us who put more stock in prayer than in Twitter. He shows how we can best understand the language of our post-Christian world without being duped by it. Read this book!"

Rosaria Butterfield, Former professor of English and Women's Studies; author of *Secret Thoughts of an Unlikely Convert*

"Christians are the intellectual outlaws under the current secular conditions. To believe the truth claims of Christianity is to defy principalities and powers—and to face an intellectual onslaught. In this context of increasing hostility to the Christian faith, Marvin Olasky's careful and theologically-informed reflection on the culture is a needed resource for the church. Olasky's new book, *World View*, is a thoughtful and rich resource for those who are seeking to walk faithfully during this challenging cultural moment."

R. Albert Mohler, Jr., President of the Southern Baptist Theological Seminary

"For years, Marvin Olasky has inspired thousands of readers to stop separating their moral principles from their politics and start thinking compassionately about those left behind in our society. This volume puts his arguments into one handy compendium. Readers of all faiths and political stripes will find inspiration here to make sure their own ethical commitments are informing how they live each day."

Arthur Brooks, President of American Enterprise Institute

"The searing truth and wisdom in these pages is vintage Marvin Olasky. And the best part of all: it rubs off. See for yourself!"

Eric Metaxas, Best-selling author of *Martin Luther: the Man Who Rediscovered God and Changed the World*

"This provocative collection is a monument to Marvin Olasky's precise, searching and devout mind. For those who share his beliefs and those who do not, Olasky will not let you rest, writing with a style that mimics what he is searching for in his writing—the balance between passionate conviction and profound compassion—with a voice that is mindful of the humility required by grace."

John Dickerson, Moderator, *Face the Nation*; author of *Whistlestop: My Favorite Stories from Campaign History*

World View

SEEKING GRACE AND TRUTH IN OUR COMMON LIFE

Marvin Olasky

New
Growth
Press

www.newgrowthpress.com

New Growth Press, Greensboro, NC 27404
Copyright © 2017 by Marvin Olasky

The contents of this book are compiled from columns that originally appeared in *World* magazine under the byline of Marvin Olasky.

Scripture quotations are taken from The Holy Bible, English Standard Version.® Copyright © 2000; 2001 by Crossway Bibles, a division of Good News Publishers. Used by permission. All rights reserved.

Cover Design: Faceout Books, faceoutstudio.com

ISBN (Print): 978-1-945270-83-3
ISBN (eBook): 978-1-945270-84-0

Library of Congress Cataloging-in-Publication Data on file

Printed in the United States of America

24 23 22 21 20 19 18 17   1 2 3 4 5

CONTENTS

Foreword

I fell in love with America in the sixth grade while reading Landmark Books, and with journalism in high school. In my mid-twenties, after a decade of jagged radicalism, I fell in love with Christ and with Susan (we've now been married for forty-one years). Many of the fifty-eight columns in this book, written from 1997 through 2016, reflect the interplay of these four loves.

This year is the 500th anniversary of the birth of the Protestant Reformation, which returned to the fore Christianity's emphasis on God's grace rather than man's works. It's the 100th anniversary of the Russian Revolution, which led to class warfare. Martin Luther understood, and Vladimir Lenin did not, that we are all weighed down by sin, and can make little progress until we recognize our own faults instead of blaming others. That sensibility also underlies many of these columns.

"American Studies," an undisciplined discipline, was both my undergraduate major and my PhD field. As the United States has become increasingly disunited, seeking grace and truth in our common life is a challenge. In a sense, I'm inspecting a roof from the top of a tall ladder buffeted by fierce winds, with my shadow obscuring many of the shingles. I generally start columns with a rough idea but not an outline, so writing comes from peering and learning rather than regurgitating a party line.

Instead of including long series of columns excavating particular concerns of mine like poverty-fighting, abortion, education, religion, or baseball, I've tried in this book to mix up the topics so as to provide an American Studies sampler. The common denominator is counter-programming: I try to wake up those who are complacent and calm down those who are frantic. My columns may make sense to some conservatives, but I hope they also reach—without any ideological kissing up—people on the left.

Jonathan Edwards in *Freedom of the Will* writes about a king and a prisoner. The king opens the jail cell and tells the incarcerated he is free to leave. The prisoner, though, hates the king. Maybe he has heard from others that the king is not trustworthy and plans to torture him if he leaves, so he stays in the cell. That's where many of my former comrades and journalistic or academic colleagues reside. We can learn to trust the king only if we go back to basics. We need to reexamine the changes, institutions, and causes we have advocated and defended. We need to conclude that we ourselves need to change.

As I learned on my own rocky path, we do not conclude this on our own. Maybe a columnist can help slightly, but our only hope lies in God's grace and the hard challenges He gives us. All of us need such prodding. Contra the 1970 song, we are not stardust and we are not golden—but God has told all who listen that "you will know the truth, and the truth will set you free." (2017)

SECTION ONE:
BASICS

Fight or flight? Ride or hide? Sometimes, it's beneficial to be a Benedict, creating a community in which Christians can grow stronger and prepare to venture forth when the tide seems ready to turn. Sometimes, we should dare to be Daniels, risking our lives in the centers of power by speaking and living truth before those who probably won't listen.

Deciding which path to take requires great discernment. Rosa Parks in 1955 became a heroine when she was a Daniel and refused to move to the back of the bus in Montgomery, Alabama. A millennium before that, Christians facing Arab raiders, in what is now central Turkey, hid in underground cities and were probably wise to do so.

My own tendency at times has been to rush in, while recognizing that those with more angelic temperaments would wait. Still, this group of columns shows my desire that evangelicals should not become applause-seekers but should seek to demonstrate a Christian worldview. I propose in this section that fiscal conservatism doesn't work without biblical moorings, and that Christians won't rescue young prodigals just by displaying an elder brother sense of duty.

The Bible shows followers of Christ how to be emphatic but compassionate, ready to be Dirty Harry Christians rather than South Park conservatives—and in the process, we should emphasize humility and humanity by neither over-using nor under-using Scripture. We're part of the American tradition of making room for others and looking for government to promote the general welfare, not provide it.

Demonstrating Christianly

You may have heard the story of the time four decades ago when President Lyndon Johnson invited reporters to his ranch for dinner. Since his press secretary Bill Moyers had seminary training, LBJ asked him to say grace. When the designated prayer spoke softly, Johnson requested that he speak up. Mr. Moyers replied, "I wasn't talking to you, Mr. President."

The focal point of that anecdote for some is LBJ's arrogance—but the late president was right. Public prayer, whether in church or at the dinner table, has two audiences, one on earth and one in heaven. Prayer tells God what He already knows but wants to hear from us, and it also may teach human listeners what we do not know but should.

Public prayer should be not only loud enough for all to hear but discerning concerning what people will hear. The goal should be to communicate with God but also to communicate about Him and His attributes, such as holiness and mercy. Thus far, I hope most readers are with me, but pay attention, because a perhaps controversial application is coming: Public demonstration by Christians should also emphasize communication about God.

When American Christian activists are riled up about something, we show our displeasure. I can do this by writing, but I've learned that while rants may make me feel temporarily better and excite others, they don't accomplish much toward helping with what's appropriately called the Great Commission: "Go therefore and make disciples of all nations."

Christ's statement at the end of Matthew's gospel is more complicated than it may seem. It specifies "baptizing them in the name of the Father and of the Son and of the Holy Spirit," so Trinitarian teaching and then a baptismal sign and seal of the faith brought about by God's grace are both important. It also emphasizes "teaching them to observe all that I commanded you," so neither a vague spirituality nor a

3

theoretical mastery is sufficient. As part of a process that lasts a lifetime, believing hearers are to become doers of God's commands.

Put all this together and we start to see what an ideal Christian protest of a political or cultural event might look like. First, its goal should not be to make the demonstrators feel righteous or more cohesive in the face of a hostile world: the Christian slogan is not, "If it feels good, do it." Second, it should communicate that God brings in people and has expectations for us—in other words, both mercy and holiness.

Let's take abortion protests as a particularly appropriate example, given the January 22, *Roe v. Wade* anniversary cover date of this issue. A Christian demonstration outside an abortion business should declare that abortion is wrong and that God is merciful to aborters and abortionists who come to faith in Him.

Protesters who seem hateful to troubled women because they appear to offer condemnation rather than hope are not helping the cause of Christ. On the other hand, a demonstration that merely offers cups of hot chocolate to women arriving for abortions on a wintry day is also sub-Christian, since demonstrators might seem like spectators at a race urging the contestants on to the finish line.

The frequent biblical metaphor of Christians as salt is apt not only because salt is both a preservative and a flavoring, but because the two elements that make up salt—NaCl, sodium and chlorine—are both poisonous when ingested by themselves. Salty protests highlight what God opposes but also show, both in words and style, what God proposes: acceptance of His mercy.

My ideal prolife demonstration at an abortion business features protesters winsomely providing information about alternatives to abortion. Our folks would not use bullhorns, which The Blues Brothers effectively linked with Nazis. Some biased souls will see Christians as loudmouths no matter how we act, but we should not make it easy for them—and if we do, we're hurting rather than helping the cause of Christ.

Our models here should be Daniel in Babylon and Paul in Greece, both of which were rife with pagan belief and practice, probably including infanticide. When Paul walked in Athens and saw the city was full of idols, he did not try to smash them. Instead, "he reasoned in the synagogue with the Jews and the devout persons, and in the marketplace every day with those who happened to be there" (Acts 17:17). (2005)

Prodigal Sons and Current Issues

As Tim Keller points out in *The Prodigal God* (Dutton, 2008), the parable of the prodigal son should have a plural in its name: sons. We all know of the younger brother's libertine living, but the elder brother has a more subtle problem: He is self-righteous and lacks joy.

Part of the evangelical political problem in contemporary America is that much of the press and public sees us as elder brothers. Sometimes we are that way in reaction to younger brothers. Sometimes younger brothers go their way in reaction to us.

In higher education, younger brother colleges are party schools that proffer sex and stimulants. Some Christian colleges try to avoid that by imposing tight rules in elder brother fashion. Those rules may lead to external conformity rather than deep belief. Both younger brother and elder brother colleges divert students from learning more about God.

In journalism, younger brother magazines ranging from *Rolling Stone* to *People* sell a continuation of younger brother college life. Elder brother reporters tend to be self-righteous fault-finders—and it's always someone else's fault. Elder brother journalism lacks love, charity, compassion, and a sense that all of us are in this mess together.

Christian publications that look only at sin among secularists can also be elder brothers.

In the realm of "social justice," younger brothers want governmental redistribution so everyone, regardless of conduct, gets part of the national inheritance. Some recipients of Washington's largesse are widows and orphans, but others are younger brothers or sisters: They should go home but do not because government checks allow them to keep destroying themselves. Elder brothers, though, wax sarcastic about wastrels while they overlook the needy. "Social justice" turns into either social universalism or Social Darwinism.

The gay rights debate is another younger vs. elder brother combat zone. While covering Manhattan's annual humongous Gay Pride parade, I didn't see any lip-locks except when the marchers observed a dozen souls from a church waving Bibles and screaming at them, "You're going to hell, sodomite" or "You're an abomination in the sight of God." The presence of elder brothers allowed younger brothers to feel self-righteous: ironically, ranting reminders about sin provided the opportunity to forget about sin.

Younger brothers who perceive self-righteousness or joylessness in their elders head toward mockery. On the Comedy Network, Jon Stewart is a snarky younger brother and Stephen Colbert pretends to be an elder as he parodies FOX's tut-tutting Bill O'Reilly. Elder brothers tend to forget that truth without love is like sodium without chloride: Poison, not salt.

What's rare on television and in life are third brothers who, because they know deeply that the Father loves them, have love for and patience with both elder and younger brothers. Third brothers, knowing God has forgiven them, are not prideful.

A third brother Christian college helps students to see that all people are made in the image of God and all people are sinners. Because of that, beauty shows up where we expect banality, and evil emerges where we anticipate excellence. At a third brother college, students become bilingual and bicultural, able to move in both Christian and secular circles without ignoring the problems of the former or the knowledge generated in the latter, through common grace.

Third brother journalism rises out of the history lecture in chapter seven of the book of Acts: Stephen, with neither an elder brother's pridefulness nor a younger brother's sarcasm, realistically emphasizes the fallenness of his people and the holiness of God. He does not seek life's meaning in the formation of or adherence to a man-made religion that sets up a code of morality.

Third brother politics is also different. The Founders fought for both liberty and virtue: Elder brothers tend to forget the former, younger brothers the latter. Third brothers know that we can never have enough laws to banish sin. They tell the truth but do not rant at abortionists and gay rights activists. They control their tongues and lungs not because killing babies and killing marriage is right, but because their goal is to change hearts.

Third brothers ask pointed questions, and here are ones for each of us to answer: Am I a younger, elder, or third brother? Can we, through God's grace, leave behind elder- and younger-brotherism? (2009)

Earnest Grace vs. South Park

A raucous red glare, bombast bursting in air . . .

That's the face and sound of media conservatism these days, as celebrated on best-seller lists, top-rated talk shows, and books like Brian Anderson's *South Park Conservatives* (Regnery, 2005). That title comes from the cable cartoon program known for its helpful ripping of political correctness but its harmful endorsement of rage and sarcasm.

These days, being a South Park conservative is in, and the working definition seems to be: Hit hard and don't worry about hitting below the belt, because there is no belt. If you counter the left's sputum with your own, talk show appearances and book contracts will follow.

What big shots endorse, little shots snort. Anderson approvingly quotes one undergraduate talking about himself and cohort members who "get drunk on weekends, have sex before marriage . . . cuss like sailors—and also happen to be conservative."

Conservative, maybe (although if South Park is our future, there won't be much to conserve). Clearly not Christian, though. Those who follow the Bible are to be firm but courteous—as the saying goes, hating the sin but loving the sinner. Christians should not adopt the bipolar belief that either you're (Michael) savage or you're a wimp.

The Christian way is to practice what New Jersey pastor Matt Ristuccia calls "earnest grace, the reassociation of sensibilities that we moderns have judged to be beyond association: specifically, passionate conviction and profound compassion. . . . [The apostle Paul was] so wonderstruck by the way God brought justice and judgment for human sin together with forgiveness and hope in the death of this Jesus, that Paul's earnestness could not help but be seasoned with grace."

That's certainly the way things oughta be—but contemporary culture does have peculiarities. Ann Coulter spoke in May at the University of Texas; I was still hanging out in New Jersey, but a perceptive Christian student I've taught, Amy McCullough, was there.

Amy reports that the first question to Coulter was, in essence, "couldn't she be a little nicer? Coulter said people don't respond to subtle reasoning; one has to 'bop them over the head' and use humor to make people see the light." She's probably right: earnestness on TV shows and during after-dinner speeches doesn't turn people on, and Ms. Coulter's rapid-fire attacks do.

But Amy also noted a rare, slow-motion answer: "When a young, conservative woman asked how Coulter could stand the awful things people said about her because of her stand on abortion, she hesitated, messed with her hair, and said: 'Well, it's the same way I don't care about anything else: Christ died for my sins and nothing else matters.' I think my jaw hit the floor."

On this subject, Coulter is right: It doesn't matter what people think about us. We know that those apart from Christ will often view Christians as fools unless God changes hearts, so the advice offered by US Supreme Court Justice Antonin Scalia is good and right: "Have the courage to have your wisdom regarded as stupidity. Be fools for Christ. And have the courage to suffer the contempt of the sophisticated world."

And yet, while it doesn't matter what people think about us, it does matter what people think about Christ. Sophisticates showed contempt toward Paul's words in Athens (Acts 17), but some listened. What if, instead of arguing logically, he had ranted? Or, despite Paul's own personality and preferences, what if Areopagus leaders had allowed only sound-and-fury acts? Should Paul have contented himself with bopping the heads of his listeners?

Amy's conclusion about Ann Coulter: "I enjoyed a lot of what she had to say. It'd be nice if she was nicer." Some of Coulter's stage persona may be an act, but do we have a culture in which she needs an act like that to break through the propaganda that suffuses so many college courses?

How would Paul act in today's culture? How, for that matter, would eighteenth-century members of the religious right like Samuel Adams and Patrick Henry? I suspect they would still be firm but courteous, displaying bravery without bombast. I'm not knocking Coulter; I only hope that she finds a way to rout liberal stereotypes without fulfilling others. She's too good to be South Park. So, for that matter, is any Christian. (2005)

New Neighbors

We worry a lot about presidential candidates, but this election is showing the need for thoughtful, hopeful voters. When voters are pessimistic and adamant about holding onto our own slices of pie, candidates respond in protectionist ways. When voters are optimistic about the opportunity to bake more pies and share the bounty, then campaigns brighten.

Churches and Christian schools that teach us to love our neighbors can grow better voters. They should teach that expansive, non-defensive Christianity has been the outstanding vehicle in human history for increasing the liberty of those seen as sub-human until Christians began viewing them as neighbors: the poor, the sick, the sexually-exploited; racial, ethnic, and religious minorities; the not-yet-born and the declining but not-yet-dead.

Sure, we have to recognize that some Christians over the centuries defended slavery or embraced nativism, but they were doing what was common in much of the world. The sensational news is that many Christians have fought for what was uncommon. American Christians with an expansive sensibility have always been the leaders in taking risks and making "We, the people" include more and more people viewed not as threats but as neighbors.

The big US experiment from the 1840s to 1924 was whether the "we" could include millions of Catholic and Jewish immigrants. Some Protestants who thought of America as a Holy Land fought what they saw as pollution by immigrants, but by the end of the century the consensus was clear: We the neighbors includes Catholics and Jews, and soon came a smattering of Buddhists, Hindus, and Muslims.

The big twentieth-century experiment was whether the "we" could include different racial and ethnic groups. Despite Constitutional amendments, the Civil War hadn't settled that, since African-Americans largely remained poor and disenfranchised. In the mid-twentieth century, though, strong and courageous Christians (once again, sadly, with exceptions) fought for civil rights as many of their predecessors had fought for emancipation.

During February, Black History Month, children in Christian schools should learn the uniqueness of our history. In India, Hindu priests lead the opposition to equal rights for the generally dark-skinned Dalits ("untouchables"). In the United States, though, ministers like Martin Luther King, Jr., and others of the Southern Christian Leadership Conference demanded to be treated as neighbors. Many Christians and Jews joined their cause.

Like or dislike his politics, it was good that Barack Obama could win in Iowa, where few African-Americans live. Like or dislike the Clintons, it's shameful that they have fought back from that initial loss by playing racial cards. While recognizing the need to control our borders, we should be sad to see some GOP candidates playing the immigration card.

America has been a land of addition, not subtraction. Social Darwinists for almost 150 years have tried to subtract the poor from the list of We the neighbors, but compassionate conservatives have insisted on treating even the homeless as part of the "we" who are capable of working, marrying, and building families.

Christians have also insisted that unborn children are part of the "we," despite the Supreme Court's exclusionary attempt in *Roe v. Wade*. In the American house are many mansions, and our history is one of finding more room than we thought there was.

One woman who had an abortion wrote in 1976, our nation's bicentennial, that "there just wasn't room" in her life for the child growing within her. Later, she realized that she could have made room. She wrote, "I have this ghost now. A very little ghost that only appears when I'm seeing something beautiful, like the full moon on the ocean last weekend. And the baby waves at me. And I wave at the baby."

In this month that brings George Washington's birthday, it's worth remembering a letter he wrote to one synagogue in 1789: "May the children of the stock of Abraham who dwell in this land continue to merit and enjoy the good will of the other inhabitants, while everyone shall sit in safety under his own vine and fig tree and there shall be none to make him afraid." That should be our continuing goal for this nation. We can make room. Christians should lead the way. (2008)

The Daniel Standard

Christians in the public square should be known not only for years of perseverance in the face of snide attacks, but also for good humor in refuting them. Some people who would like to stand for Christ become irate, even despairing, but the Bible gives us confidence—in part, by showing how believers have been a harassed minority before, and how God was faithful.

Past circumstances were often far more difficult than those we now face. The last chapter of Second Chronicles, for example, tells how the Babylonians 2,600 years ago "broke down the wall of Jerusalem." Israelites had lived in a land where every aspect of life was to point them to the holiness of one God who reigned above all. Suddenly, they found themselves exiled to Babylon: instant culture shock.

Babylonia then was a land of many gods where almost anything was allowed as long as it did not interfere with obeying and paying tribute to the king. Some Israelites probably sequestered themselves as much as they could from Babylonian civilization. But the book of Daniel tells of how he and a few other young men enrolled in a three-year course designed to leave them with an MBA—Master of Babylonian Arts. It also describes how he came to prominence when God gave him the grace to comprehend and interpret a dream of King Nebuchadnezzar.

Training and grace were related. Providentially, Daniel had gained the understanding of Babylonian culture that he needed to communicate powerfully the essence of the dream. He told the king of a great statue broken into pieces by a stone cut from a mountain by no human hand. That stone then "became a great mountain and filled the whole earth."

Daniel, knowing how Babylonians saw mountains either as gods or the abode of gods, then explained that the powerful stone came from not a mere mountain god but from "the God of heaven [who] will set up a kingdom that shall never be destroyed" (Daniel 2:44). Nebuchadnezzar, in turn, gained a vision of the mightiness of this God and told Daniel, "Truly your God is God of gods and Lord of kings" (v.47).

Nebuchadnezzar made Daniel ruler over the central part of the Babylonian Empire, and the Israelite in succeeding decades was in and out of the Babylonian court. He spoke forthrightly to Nebuchadnezzar by telling his patron that he would become insane for seven years. Daniel, forgotten by a second king, came back just in time to predict the kingdom's imminent fall. Later, conspirators used Daniel's regular prayer habits against him in a way that led to his being thrown to lions. God then delivered Daniel and so impressed a third king, Darius, that the monarch recognized "the God of Daniel" as "the living God, enduring forever."

That's the highlight reel of Daniel's seven decades in or close to government: Much of the time, it appears, those in power ignored him. Patient Daniel, faithful to biblical understanding but comprehending Babylon, is a role model for Christians who want to work in the dominant culture of America but not be of it. Daniel's life was not easy—at least twice it almost ended prematurely—and he spent his entire career among people of different beliefs. But he challenged those beliefs by standing for God decade after decade, and we can do the same. He had to be bilingual and bicultural, and so should we be.

We know that not only from the example of Daniel, but from God's command. The prophet Jeremiah wrote (chapter 29, verses 4–7), "Thus says the LORD of Hosts, the God of Israel, to all the exiles whom I sent into exile from Jerusalem to Babylon: 'Build houses and live in them; plant gardens and eat their produce. . . . Seek the welfare of the city where I have sent you into exile, and pray to the LORD on its behalf, for in its welfare you will find your welfare.'"

To understand and apply Jeremiah's teaching, we need to understand that in his day Babylon was not the symbol of everything wicked that it had become by the time John wrote the book of Revelation. In Jeremiah's time some Babylonians were probably good neighbors, trading gardening tips—and that's how life is in America today. Our situation is different in one respect: America, unlike Babylonia, started out on a biblical base. But now the parallels are great, and so are the opportunities: That was a good time for gutsy Daniels, and so is ours. (2003)

Political Humility

No one had to sign a statement of faith before tossing British tea into Boston Harbor in 1773. No one has to sign a statement of faith before joining a Tea Party demonstration in 2010. And therein lies a lesson for politically involved Christians.

As Christians, we want to defend our religious liberty. Parents should be able to homeschool their children or send them to Christian schools. Christian professors and social workers, when asked what animates them, should be able to talk about Christ. Adoption agencies based on biblical understandings should be able to place children with father-mother rather than same-sex couples.

But we should also, as citizens, be involved with issues such as health care. Nothing in the Bible explicitly says we can't have government-controlled health care. Nothing in the Bible says we can't have monarchy, for that matter. So we get into trouble when we band together as Christians and speak dogmatically on issues that aren't clearly connected to our faith. On extra-biblical policy matters we should speak as citizens and join with other citizens in seeking a redress of grievances.

We can gain wisdom here by studying Paul's first letter to the Corinthians. Look at the phrases he uses: "Now as a concession, not a command, I say this . . . I say (I, not the Lord) . . . I have no command from the Lord, but I give my judgment . . . in my judgment." If Paul, an apostle who wrote under God's inspiration, is this cautious, how much more careful should the rest of us be?

The same goes in the classroom and the public square. Long-time readers of *World* are familiar with the whitewater rapids metaphor we use in determining how we approach news coverage. Class 1 and Class 2 rapids are easy to navigate, so Class 1 issues are those on which the Bible explicitly takes a position (for example, murder and adultery are wrong). On Class 1 issues we take a clear, biblical stand. For example, we don't try to balance pro-abortion and pro-life viewpoints. Class 2 issues involve an implicit biblical position (for example, parents should give their children a Bible-based education).

But God, for His purposes, has given us in most of the Bible not a detailed instruction manual but a narrative history of particular actions at particular times. The book of Joshua reports wars of extermination: Are we to go and do likewise? The story-telling in Judges 17—after a mother enables her thieving son, he sets up a cult and hires an unethical Levite—is masterful, but the teaching is not as direct as "Thus saith the Lord."

Clarity decreases with other rapids classes. Class 3 stories are those in which partisans of both sides can quote scriptural verses, but careful study allows biblical conclusions. Welfare reform is an example: Partisans of government entitlements rightly cite biblical verses about helping the poor, but it's also important to bring out biblical teaching about the challenging, personal, and spiritual way in which compassion should be applied.

Some issues are Class 4, where we apply biblical teaching about human nature and learn from biblical history. Others are Class 5, where the Bible doesn't give us guidance but we can learn much from extra-biblical history. For example, we have reason to be suspicious of the person who says, "I'm from the government and I'm here to help you." The higher the class, the more we are likely to report on various viewpoints but not take a strong position ourselves.

Class 6 issues are those in which there is no clear biblical position nor other clear indications, so people equally well-versed in the Bible will often take diametrically opposed positions. Technical economic issues—whether to raise or lower interest rates, for example—are often of this nature, as are complex questions of international diplomacy. Christians should be careful not to state that there is one biblical position on this subject to which all should ascribe, or else.

We should fight the tendency among liberal Christians to think that every issue is a Class 5 or 6. Discerning Christians who have immersed themselves in the Bible can paddle aggressively through most rapids without ending up in freezing water. Christ did not die for us so that we would be captives of fear. At the same time, it's important to remember that God has not spoken on every subject: Class 1 and 2 issues should be clear to all, but the others require considerable discernment and humility in staking out a claim. (2010)

Dates that Will Live in Infamy

In *The Death's Head Chess Club*, a new novel by John Donoghue, chess player Emil arrives at the Auschwitz concentration camp with his family. Soon his wife is in one line for women able to work. He is with men able to work. His two small sons, with their grandmother, are in a third line.

The scene continues: "Emil is anxious about his two boys, but the officer tells him not to worry . . . the children will be sent to the family camp, where they will be cared for by those who are too old for manual labor. He says it with the weary calmness of a man who has given this reassurance a hundred times before. It has the ring of normality, of truth. But . . . in Auschwitz, 'family' means death."

Guards march away the children and the aged. "Emil mouths a quiet 'Au revoir' to his children. 'Be good for Granny.' He does not know he will never see them again." They and Grandma go to the gas chamber and then "up the chimney," as their corpses are burned. Months later, Emil is "crying, inconsolably. 'My children, my children,' he wails. . . . My beautiful boys . . . I don't even have a photograph of them. I can't remember what they look like.'"

Six million Jews died, and others as well. This year we're on track to hit 60 million aborted babies since the *Roe v. Wade* decision on January 22, 1973. Ten times as many. The four-year Holocaust began in earnest in 1941, when German armies headed east and Einsatzgruppen paramilitary units conducted mass shootings of Jews, probably including my great-grandparents. We're now at forty-four years since *Roe v. Wade*, eleven times as many.

If you're an abortion advocate and you're reading this now, you're probably angry at such a comparison. You might point out that pro-life people generally allow for abortion in those (very rare) cases when it's needed to save the life of the mother. You might point out that the penalties for abortionists when their practice was illegal were not the same as the penalties for murdering born humans.

And I'd agree with you that the Holocaust in its wholesale evil—crowding men, women, and children into a closed room and wafting in poison gas—provides a more brutal picture than the current abortion retail trade, where an unborn child floats peacefully in protected space, until needles and knives suddenly invade.

Nevertheless, think of what Samantha Power, concluding her time as US Ambassador to the UN, said last month as parents holding babies in blood-soaked blankets picked their way past corpses in the streets of Aleppo, Syria. She asked the Assad regime and its Russian enablers, "Are you truly incapable of shame? Is there literally nothing that can shame you? Is there no act of barbarism against civilians, no execution of a child, that gets under your skin, that just creeps you out a little bit?"

We should say not only to abortionists but to all their enablers—justices, politicians, propagandists, and bystanders—what Powers said: "Denying or obfuscating the facts, as you will do today—saying up is down, black is white—will not absolve you. When one day there is a full accounting of the horrors committed in this assault of Aleppo [substitute: abortion]—and that day will come, sooner or later—you will not be able to say you did not know what was happening. You will not be able to say you were not involved. We all know what is happening. And we all know you are involved."

As many have said, a single death is a tragedy, a thousand deaths a statistic—but at some point big numbers become grotesque. Six million Holocaust deaths. Sixty million US abortions. An estimated 56 million induced abortions worldwide each year. When do those numbers creep us out—at least a little bit? "My beautiful boys," Emil mourns: "I can't remember what they look like." We do know what aborted babies cut apart in their sanctuaries look like.

January 20, 1942: That's when senior Nazi officials met in the Berlin suburb of Wannsee and planned what they thought would be the "Final

Solution of the Jewish question." January 22, 1973: That's when seven Supreme Court justices agreed to the mass killing of unborn children. Now cemented: the infamy of those two dates. Still being poured: this January's cement. What kind of a sidewalk do we hope to see? (2017)

Whose Applause?

Christians who have adopted the slogan "family first" as a euphemism for biblical morality might be surprised to see how frequently the Bible puts family second.

Look, for example, at chapter 8 of Luke, when Jesus's mother and brothers, thinking He is out of His mind, ask to see Him. Jesus replies, "My mother and my brother are those who hear the word of God and do it" (v. 21).

Look at Luke 9, when a man says, "I will follow you, Lord, but let me first say farewell to those at my home." Jesus replies, "No one who puts his hand to the plow and looks back is fit for the kingdom of God" (vv. 61–62).

Look at Luke 11, when a woman cries out, "Blessed is the womb that bore you, and the breasts at which you nursed!" Jesus replies, "Blessed are those who hear the word of God and keep it!" (vv. 27–28).

What's going on here? Is Jesus dissing His mom? Clearly not: Christ was without sin. But He was also without the sin of yearning for the favor of others—even parents—who cheer what is not godly.

Parents are our first applauders. As children, we desperately yearn for their approbation, and to some extent that sticks with us for life. Jesus is not only our elder brother in rising from the dead, but in showing us how to place God's kind words (well done, good and faithful servant) above even those of our parents, and certainly above those social arbiters who may decide that we are hopelessly dorky.

The willingness to forego applause from society's trend-setters distinguishes tough Christians from the Mr. Pliables of the world. That independent spirit also seems to characterize Supreme Court Justices

Clarence Thomas and Antonin Scalia; to their credit, they do not seem to care how they are treated in *The Washington Post*.

Pressures to flip come daily. A Christian student taking a test or writing a term paper to be read by an adversarial professor has to count the cost of being on the Lord's side: "I may be graded down." A Christian humanities or social sciences professor writing an article has to count the cost: "If I am a fool for Christ, my colleagues will consider me a just plain fool." A Christian talking to her non-Christian parent has to count the cost: "If I talk about Jesus, my mom will think I'm weird."

None of this is to say that we should be personally obnoxious: Whether we are presenting the gospel or a Bible-based political position, we should search out points of contact. Furthermore, we should be prepared to meet and talk with all kinds of people, just as Jesus ate and taught all kinds.

But, when crunch time comes, as it always does, we must not shrink from asking ourselves, whose applause do I covet? Do I desperately want to become a member of a certain club? If necessary, we need to give up first parental applause, and then the prizes offered by those who place other gods before God.

Garrison Keillor recently contrasted Minneapolis, which he says wants to be hip, with its twin city St. Paul, apparently content to be square. Keillor wrote that "Minneapolis, not St. Paul, is a mecca for performance artists, people who can't sing or dance or write or act but who can crawl through a pile of truck tires wearing a shower curtain. . . . Minneapolitans lean forward and watch them, perspiring, afraid that some subtlety may escape them. St. Paulites look at each other and say, 'Whose idea was this?'"

As I look at new Bible translations that appear to give in to feminist pressures, I ask, "Whose idea was this?" And I think of how the original St. Paul gave a hip performance for a while in Acts 17, impressing the elite of Athens. But then—inexplicably, by worldly standards—he blew it by talking about the resurrection of the dead. Several Athenians did come to believe, but Paul gave up his opportunity to win broad Areopagus acclaim.

Every Christian intellectual, every Christian journalist, every Christian Bible translator these days, faces that same temptation: Do I become (within the Keillor framework) a Minneapolitan, or do I stick with St. Paul? (1997)

Provide vs. Promote

In the mid-1990s Bill Clinton, going with the flow, announced that the era of big government is over. Here in December 2001, liberals and neo-conservatives are saying the easy US victory in the first stage of the war on terrorism shows the merits of a big government. That's illogical spin.

We can puncture the balloon of those who would use military needs to engorge government generally by learning from the original Cassius Clay of Kentucky. Some may remember that name as Muhammad Ali's pre-Muslim moniker, but I'm referring to the antebellum anti-slavery editor and politician who faced many hostile crowds. In the 1840s he typically picked up a Bible and said, "To those who respect God's Word, I appeal to this book." Then he held up a copy of the Constitution and said, "To those who respect our fundamental law, I appeal to this document." Then he took out two pistols and his Bowie knife and said, "To those who recognize only force . . ."

Conservatives today should adopt an updated Cassius Clay posture, with three arguments—Bible, Constitution, and a readiness for political skirmish—deployed as necessary. Let's start with the Bible, which is clear on government's proper function. Biblically, government's chief role is to wield "the power of the sword" against both external enemies and internal criminals. Government is needed to terrorize terrorists and other evil-doers, so soldiers, cops, and judges are needed. The role of government, though, is not to construct a new Eden or reconstruct society by using its power to redistribute income.

The prophet Samuel was among those who realistically examined the tendencies of government and issued a warning about what a king would do: "He will take the best of your fields and vineyards and olive orchards and give them to his servants. He will take the tenth of your grain and of your vineyards and give it to his officers and to his servants. He will take your male servants and your female servants and the best of your young men and your donkeys, and put them to his work. He will take the tenth of your flocks, and you shall be his slaves" (1 Samuel 8:14–17).

Those Bible lessons are important, but many Americans believe we have outgrown them. The Preamble to the Constitution, though, makes a memorable distinction: the federal government exists to "provide for the common defense" and to "promote the general welfare." There's a huge difference between providing and promoting; the choice of those particular words was not accidental.

"Providing" means doing the job yourself. The government has an army. Religious organizations, the Lions Club, and the American Atheist Union do not have armies, because Washington's job is to provide for the common defense. "Promoting" means developing a favorable environment within which others are likely to step up. The federal government was not involved in poverty-fighting during the nineteenth century, but American churches, synagogues, businesses, and civic and fraternal associations fought a war on poverty then that was far more effective than our capital-W War of the 1960s and 1970s.

It is constitutionally right to grow a big government for defense when we have potent adversaries abroad. It is constitutionally wrong to grow a big government for welfare, especially since civil society can accomplish many of the tasks that government has taken upon itself. We have lots of ways now to promote the general welfare; my favorite is to establish a $500 tax credit for contributions to anti-poverty groups. Each taxpayer could send a check for $500 to a group he saw as effective, and take that money right off his taxes. President Bush proposed a version of that during his presidential campaign, but it lost out in the post-inaugural shuffle.

All Americans should learn the Constitutional distinction between providing and promoting. Yet what if proponents of big government for domestic purposes pay attention neither to the Bible or the Constitution? Then conservatives will have to wage tough but peaceful political warfare, or a government that defeats terrorists may turn to terrorizing its own citizens. Cassius Clay used his Bowie knife, but we will need a president who uses the bully pulpit to fight for spending that is needed and to fight against that which benefits the princes of Washington but turns other citizens into paupers. (2001)

Yes, Kristin, Many Careers Can Glorify God

Dear Editor,
   During these past few months, my heart has been very burdened to reclaim America for Christ. With each additional school shooting, every murder of an unborn baby, my heart is convicted that this nation is in very serious trouble. How much longer will the Lord withhold His wrath?

I feel that it is my responsibility as a Christian to do something, but I am not quite sure what I should do. I am writing you in hopes you can help direct me to a career that would be effective in bringing America back to Christ.

Kristin Morgan
Home school student

Dear Kristin,
   It certainly makes sense to be sad about what's happening in America. It's good to see our great need for Christ's speedy return and the judgment that will come.

Some people even say that there's no use thinking about training for careers as doctors, lawyers, or journalists—that all of us should spend every minute of every day directly proclaiming the gospel to all with whom we come in contact.

It's no use, they say, planning long-term, because the Lord through storms, plagues, Y2K bugs, or whatever, will soon destroy this culture. America deserves God's wrath and curse, and the end is near.

Kristin, we do deserve God's wrath and curse. We always do. And yet, the Lord is merciful to us, and He's been merciful to our culture despite abundant sin. Maybe the bowl of his wrath is filling up, but it seems that He has an enormous bowl, and we don't know how close or how far from pouring it may be.

So you're right to prepare for decades to come, not merely days. As Christians we are in exile from our real home, and we should take to heart the verses in chapter 29 of Jeremiah that contain the great prophet's letter to the Jewish exiles in Babylon: "Build houses and settle down; plant gardens and eat what they produce. Marry and have sons and daughters . . ."

Kristin, you're right to note that it is your responsibility as a Christian to do something—but it is not your responsibility to do everything. If you build a house, plant a garden, marry, and have children—that is good. If you seek a career that will be effective in bringing America back to Christ, you may be sorely disappointed, because perhaps America will not come back to Christ. But you have a choice of many careers in which you can glorify God, and in the process perhaps help to bring some Americans to Christ.

Ask what gifts has God given you—because He does not waste talents. If you're good in math, think about being an engineer. If you like science and can stand the sight of blood, think about being a doctor. If you're a good writer, by all means think of being a journalist, because we desperately need people who can apply biblical wisdom to the events around us.

Kristin, I don't want to direct you to a career based on what I like, and I don't want you to direct yourself to a career just based on what you like. Instead, you—with parents and pastors and friends—should inventory your talents and discern the career that God is directing you to. Take your likes and dislikes into account also, because our chief purpose in life is to glorify God and enjoy Him forever (and forever begins right now). But look particularly at what you're good at, because over the long run you'll like the godly pleasure that true achievement brings.

In the next few years, don't think it's up to you to save America: it's up to God. The words of God that Jeremiah relayed to ancient Israel are relevant to us: "Seek the welfare of the city where I have sent you into exile, and pray to the LORD on its behalf, for in its welfare you will find your welfare" (Jeremiah 29:7).

Above all, Kristin, pray for the victims of sin in America, but do not worry. Psalm 131 has a wonderful message for not only theological study but everyday living: "I do not occupy myself with things too great or marvelous for me. But I have calmed and quieted my soul, like a weaned child with its mother; like a weaned child is my soul within me" (vv. 1–2).

As we approach Thanksgiving, even with all the things that are bad in America, we have so much to thank God for. Psalm 131 instructs us on how to be thankful every day, and its last line tells us what to do today and tomorrow: "O Israel, hope in the LORD from this time forth and forevermore." (1999)

[Kristin is now a member of the *World* editorial staff—and I had always wanted to write a "Yes, Virginia, there is a Santa Claus" letter.]

SECTION TWO: CHANGES

The second act of five-act plays is often where we learn the depth of the abyss into which characters are plunging. A look at the gods worshipped on the altars of American culture shows our time of troubles has begun. From the dream factories of Hollywood to the misery factories of the poverty-industrial complex, the wood is rotten, but we only seem able to smooth some rough edges.

One basic problem: From the Supreme Court to confused kids, radical autonomy is the rage. Christians raise hackles if we point out shackles—but we're called to do so in our era of insecurity. Millennials often want to be rolling stones, postponing marriage and children until they've matured and established themselves—but marriage and children are key God-given helps in becoming mature.

Updating the Jewish tradition, I see wise sons as liberty-appreciating romantic realists, and wicked sons jailing themselves and others in a suffocating materialism. The diminishing of discrimination is mostly a plus, but if people merely move the bottom rail to the top, we enact revenge—not renewal. Secularists shouldn't contradict their ideology by searching for human messiahs, yet they repeatedly do so—and then feel fooled.

An Era of Insecurity

Søren Kierkegaard wrote sardonically that the history of the world is the history of boredom, which he called "the root of all evil. . . . The gods were bored; therefore they created human beings." Adam's boredom led to Eve, Eve's boredom led to snake-listening, Cain's boredom led to murder, more boredom led to Babel, and so on.

Far be it from me to contradict the Danish philosopher, but an amusing-ourselves-to-death America these days may be characterized less by boredom than by anger. Dana Milbank of *The Washington Post*, a self-described "left-leaning reporter," asked late last month, "Why is the left still so angry?" He reviewed 1,800 comments posted about his columns and concluded that "even under Obama, the anger on the left is, if anything, more personal and vitriolic than on the right."

Why? Milbank quoted one analyst: "People get used to being angry and when things change, they don't. So they find stuff to be mad about." True, and not just about the present. For millennia, many people have been used to being angry: Look at all the wars. Maybe we have so much fighting because of boredom, but I see it as the result of sin multiplied by social insecurity, one result of the fall of man. Adam and Eve were at first secure in every way in the garden, but many of their descendants for millennia were spiritually and materially impoverished—and angry.

The second half of the twentieth century became for many Americans an unprecedented era of material security. My father-in-law spent his whole working life at Ford. Millions of others had similar careers. Professors could gain tenure. Journalists could have steady jobs. Blue-collar workers had unions. Farmers had price supports. The elderly gained Social Security and Medicare. Antibiotics and medical improvements ended epidemics that once left parents burying most of their children.

Since change in the right amount is invigorating, employment security had an economic and social downside, and life itself was not fully secure. Some children still died. Cancer threatened. Accidents happened. Cold War possibilities were nightmarish. No matter what precautions we took, the ultimate insecurity of death would soon leave all staring into nothingness, apart from the hope that faith in God allows.

Nevertheless, many people felt generally secure. Workers in Europe and Japan, which continued to emphasize employment for life even as the practice began to die in America, whistled even more loudly past the graveyard. Such security also had a political impact: Communist parties withered. Margaret Thatcher in the 1980s argued logically that turning renters into homeowners would increase the Conservative vote.

So what has happened in our brave new century? In 2001 a day of horror led to the creation of the Department of Homeland Security, the name itself generated by insecurity. Lifetime corporate employment is gone. Newspapers are dinosaurs. New colleges don't have tenure. Social Security is insecure. And now, amid recession, many jobs are gone and others going.

Not that there isn't plenty of anger on the right, and not that wives are always secure, but consider: Most married women voters in recent presidential elections have favored Republican candidates, most never-married or divorced women voters have gone Democratic. Not that home-owning is always secure (just look at the recent forfeitures), but homeowners recently have been more likely to vote Republican, and apartment-dwellers have shaded Democratic. The correlation of material insecurity and leftward leanings makes sense, because the left wants the government to make us feel secure.

Both security and insecurity, by themselves, create problems. Moscow waiters often were, and tenured professors often are, contemptuous toward those who pay the bills or make sure they're paid—customers, parents, executives. Those without long-term contracts are often jumpy, suspicious of administrators, fearing plots where there are none.

Experience in Japan, Europe, and some large US corporations suggests that security often engenders complacency.

If neither material security nor insecurity work, what's the solution? The same as to virtually every problem in the world: faith in Christ. Since we're sinners, we're all prone to insecurity, unless we realize that our security is not subjective but objective, not dependent on what we do but on what Christ has done. We feel secure when we know deep down that all things work together for the good of those who believe in Him. Some might scoff: Superficial answer? No. There's nothing deeper. (2009)

A Pro-Choice Culture

Maybe it's because, as a professor, I deal with lots of twenty-year-olds. Maybe it's because I live in Austin, a charmingly weird town. But here's something I'll say straight out, and then wait for the slings and arrows of outraged readers: Much of the conservative Christian rhetoric we hear today misses the mark because it is both too hard and too soft.

I've seen over the years that many college students cannot grasp moral arguments. If we say, in relation to abortion or many other issues, "Thou shalt do X because it's the right thing to do," blank stares or incredulous glances result. Moral absolutes resonate poorly among students who desire absolute freedom and have never heard G. K. Chesterton's wise reminder: "The point of having an open mind, like having an open mouth, is to close it on something solid."

This is generally bad news, but here's a silver (or at least rhinestone) lining: In our prochoice culture, home schooling can expand, school vouchers have a fighting chance, addicts can be offered faith-based along with conventionally liberal anti-addiction programs, and creation can be taught alongside evolution. Name the political debate, and the winner most often is he who talks of expanding choices rather than restricting them. Sometimes, that bias will help Bible-based ideas gain a foothold.

Furthermore, since we are not to put our trust in princes, it makes sense for Christian believers to be political skeptics, particularly in relation to three decades of Washington orthodoxy. Liberal true believers for years thought they had all the right answers. Poverty? Redistribute

income. Crime? Push for gun control. Kids in trouble? Build self-esteem. Crisis pregnancies? Abort.

Yet, since God created the world and knows what works best for
His creatures to live happily in it, a lot of politically correct activities
are pragmatically incorrect. Pro-aborts, ignoring the personhood of the
unborn child, want everything to depend on the mother's situation.
OK, let's compare the physical and psychological condition of aborting
moms with those who place their children for adoption. Hard as giving
away a live child is, meditating on a dead one is worse.

Pragmatism has its limitations, though: What if sociological testing (which cannot get at spiritual consequences) concluded that women
were better off after abortions than after years of unmarried single-parenting? Would abortion then be justified? Of course not, because life is
at stake—and here is where moral principles trump today's pro-choice
ethos. How, then, do we get to a position where Americans, trained
though most of us are in pro-choice thinking, are able to put it aside?

Let's go back to my original thesis statement: Much of the conservative Christian rhetoric we hear today misses the mark because it is both
too hard and too soft. I've described how rhetoric about right and wrong
sounds too hard in a pro-choice society. But this doesn't mean Christians should give up; instead, we need to realize that many Americans
will discard the pro-choice faith only if and when they come to Christ.

Churches hold the keys to the kingdom and also the keys to political and social change here and now. Faith in God logically requires
assent to the proposition that God is wiser than us, and that should
mean signing onto the whole Bible not picking and choosing among
doctrines. Long ago Augustine said, "If you believe in the gospel what
you like, and reject what you don't like, it is not the gospel you believe,
but yourself." Those who convert to Christianity should also convert
to a style of thinking opposed to the self-worship that underlies many
aspects of pro-choice thought.

Successful politicians build coalitions within a pro-choice culture,
but ministers must be willing to offend. It is folly to tell political leaders
that they must be bold and courageous when so many leaders within
the church are not. Yet much of what comes from major pulpits is soft,
man-pleasing rhetoric more worthy of a politician than a preacher. For

that reason, many who accept Christ as savior have no idea what it makes to take him as Lord, and they never fully move away from self-worship.

One final note: it's better to set young minds in the right path than to redirect them later. Kids who attend good Christian schools and home schools or whose parents are involved and engaged with what they're learning in public schools can learn to think biblically and to value moral argumentation. If such schooling is fruitful and multiplies, and if conversion of adults increases, our entire society will change. Until then, like it or not, we live in a pro-choice culture. (1999)

It's a Big World

You can bet that some commencement speaker this spring has said or will say in a speech what we're taught in song: "It's a small world, after all." The standard line is that improved travel and communication are showing billions of people that we're all the same.

Actually, the opposite is true: the world remains huge and is getting larger as individuals assert diverse religious views and carve out specialty occupations, avocations, and lifestyles.

The world is expanding because of economic advance. Hundreds of millions of people now are free to plow new furrows rather than work the family farm. Three centuries ago daily economic life for almost all people was similar: Rainfall, wildlife, and the quality of land varied, but farmers in all those places could readily understand what their counterparts were doing. Now, we have thousands of different callings.

The world has also become vaster and we've learned more about differences in religion. More people now know that Islam is very different from Christianity not only in its theology but its anthropology. Muslims see humans as naturally good and able to attain heaven by following the rules. Many Muslims see some humans as godlike, able to bring together in their own persons (as Muhammad supposedly did) political, military, and religious excellence.

A few journalists have noted that it's a big world. For his book *The New New Journalism*, Robert Boynton asked writer Susan Orlean, "What kinds of subjects are you drawn to?" She talked about "the profile I did about a gospel group. It was astonishing for me to glimpse a world that was so fully developed—with its own stars, sagas, myths, history, millions of devotees—that I, in my narrow life, had no idea existed."

The problem is that many journalists, unlike Orlean, lead narrow lives. One, Lawrence Wright, acknowledged this in Boynton's book: "Reporters rarely take beliefs seriously . . . the whole idea of belief is a little repugnant to them." He added, "When they are confronted with someone who is genuinely captivated by belief, reporters take pity on them by not writing about their beliefs."

Maybe that's because only ten percent of reporters and editors at leading publications attend religious services weekly (compared to forty percent among the general public). Furthermore, attenders favor generally theologically liberal churches or synagogues where they are unlikely to see beliefs changing lives. It's no surprise that reporters, as a friendly gesture, leave out belief: In describing an otherwise attractive person with a huge pimple, why emphasize the pimple?

Sometimes "small world" journalists do note theological differences, but in an "oh, by the way" manner. For example, the [Jacksonville] *Florida Times-Union* stated that "Muslims believe in all of God's prophets, including Jesus Christ. However, they believe Muhammad was the last and final prophet." Oh, that's all? What about Christ being not just one among many prophets, but God's only Son?

"Big world" journalists—and Christians should learn enough about other religions, cultures, and peoples to lead the way—can perform a major service by pointing out that people of different religions have very different beliefs about God, and that those beliefs have consequences.

For example, Muslim yearning for a caliph, a new Muhammad perfect in every realm, does not allow for the separation of powers that is needed to keep democracy from becoming tyrannical.

Commencement speakers can speak sweet nothings and no one dies. But if a presidential candidate says or implies that it's a small world after all, don't vote for him. What he doesn't understand about other religions and societies could kill us.

And what about this curious detail: that two billion people from a vast variety of cultures now pay at least a little attention to one particular crucifixion that occurred on a hill in a small country 2,000 years ago?

We need more curious journalists like Susan Orlean, who said, "I have a kind of missionary zeal to tell my readers that the world is a more complex place than they ever thought." (2007)

Apologetics in a Land with Hundreds of Worldviews

I'm beginning this column about apologetics with an apology: a heartfelt "sorry" to all the people I've sat next to on airplanes, occasionally exchanging words about going to Atlanta but not about going to heaven. I'm no master of defending the faith. Any successes I've had in helping others to focus on what's most important have been accidental (seems that way to me) and utterly foreordained (by God).

What I can report, based on everything I've heard from students, is that things have changed. God bless the methods of Campus Crusade (excuse me, Cru), but the name change is organizational recognition that we're no longer in the 1950s and 1960s. That's when most Americans had only three television channels to choose from and, in essence, three worldview alternatives—Christianity, atheism, or apathy.

From the late 1960s through the early 1990s, UHF and then cable television emerged. Meanwhile, existentialism became more than a French fancy and nihilism more than a German nightmare. Eastern religions started to make inroads. Americans suddenly had dozens of TV channels from which to choose, and the apologetic methods of Francis Schaeffer contrasted biblical approaches with dozens of worldviews.

Schaeffer, instead of focusing on the four spiritual laws, proposed that months of study and discussion could lead students to truth, through God's grace. In *The God Who Is There*, *Escape from Reason*, and other books, Schaeffer showed how biblical objectivity is true and reasonable, and the alternative is nothingness and despair. Schaeffer was God's instrument in changing the lives of hundreds in person, and then hundreds of thousands through books and films.

But change did not stop in the early 1990s. The past two decades have brought us hundreds of channels for specialty interests and millions of different religious choices. That's because "Sheilaism," named after a young nurse, has become our national religion. In their 1985 book *Habits of the Heart*, Robert Bellah and Richard Madsen, quoted "Sheila" saying, "I believe in God. I'm not a religious fanatic. . . . It's Sheilaism. Just my own little voice. . . . It's just try to love yourself and be gentle with yourself."

Bellah and Madsen called Sheilaism "a perfectly natural expression of current American religious life" that created the logical possibility "of over 220 million American religions, one for each of us." They may have underestimated the quantity—we now have more than 300 million Americans—but were right on the central impulse: To be free from the past, with its creeds, confessions, denominations, propositions, and senses of antithesis.

When many young Americans are primarily yearning for freedom, talk about objective truth may swim right by them. That's why some of the most successful pastors with young people start out not by talking about truth but about freedom. Tim Keller in Manhattan, for example, tells his youthful audience: "You may think you're free, but you're not. In shunning Christ you have made yourself a slave to money, or sex, or to a particular body image, or success, or . . . something."

Those who shun Christ embrace slavery of some kind. Those who embrace Christ gain freedom: as Jesus said to the Jews who believed him, "You will know the truth, and the truth will set you free." The University of Texas at Austin and many other institutions have carved onto administration buildings those words from John 8:32, but I have yet to see on the walls Christ's follow-ups: "Everyone who practices sin is a slave to sin," and "If the Son sets you free, you will be free indeed" (John 8:34, 36).

We need all those verses and we need to get the order right, because truth leads to freedom yet freedom does not necessarily lead to truth. Sadly, college professors these days typically advocate freedom and skip over the means by which we gain it—so students often do the same. That leads to my apologetics question: Is it unproductive to talk about eternal life with young people who don't yet care about it? Or to talk about Truth with those who don't think it exists? Why not talk about our shackles and how Christ breaks them? (2013)

The Rolling Stone Era

Fifty years ago the two greatest songs of all time (so the magazine *Rolling Stone* declared in 2004) emerged, just one month apart. The Rolling Stones' "I Can't Get No Satisfaction" (#2) came out in June, 1965. Bob Dylan's "Like a Rolling Stone" (#1) emerged in July.

That's three rolling stones in one paragraph, and that same year public policy rolled erratically, as if our legislators were stoned. The US curved toward the debtors' prison that now looms, as Medicare, Medicaid, and a variety of Great Society entitlement programs zipped through the most liberal Congress of the seven decades from 1939 through 2008. But the two greatest songs show an even wider cultural swing.

Dylan's song describes life in a meaningless world. He asked how it felt to be without a home, like a complete unknown. Dylan knew that fine clothes and a fine school are a vanity of vanities. He saw the frowns of jugglers and clowns. He knew what the writer of Ecclesiastes wrote 3,000 years ago: all things under the sun are full of weariness.

The Stones' "Satisfaction" was about more than sex. Mick Jagger and others could readily attain momentary physical pleasure, but contentment in daily life—"when I'm driving in my car . . . when I'm watchin' my TV"—eluded them. Life seemed meaningless (and the advent of no-fault divorce and fault-filled but legal abortion soon undercut two big satisfactions for most people, marriage and family).

Underlying both songs was the perceived absence of God. In October 1965, *Time* reported on the tendency of trendy academics to construct an anemic theology without God. The magazine followed up six months later with an all-black cover featuring three words in red, Is God Dead? The *Los Angeles Times* in 1968 called that startlegram one of "10 magazine covers that shook the world."

The *Time* cover provoked 3,500 letters to the editor, the most in the magazine's history. Other magazines went with the flow. Easter in 1969 was on April 6, so that's when *Newsweek* tried to increase its newsstand sales with a cover story headlined (in red letters on a black background) "The Decline and Fall of Christian America." *Time* tried to increase its Christmas sales later that year with a December 26 cover story that asked, "Is God Coming Back to Life?"

Director/screenwriter Roman Polanski understood what the purported death of God meant: In his 1968 film *Rosemary's Baby*, set in 1965, Polanski had protagonist Rosemary Woodhouse (played by Mia Farrow) picking up the "Is God Dead?" issue of *Time* in a doctor's waiting room. Many critics have called *Rosemary's Baby*, with its depiction of a woman pregnant with Satan's child, the top horror film of all time—and a life without God is certainly meaningless at best and horrifying much of the time.

Songs, magazines, and movies led the way. The Supreme Court soon went with the flow with its *Roe v. Wade* ruling in 1973, but didn't spell out the philosophy behind it until another abortion decision in 1992: In *Planned Parenthood v. Casey*, Justice Anthony Kennedy wrote that "at the heart of liberty is the right to define one's own concept of existence, of the universe, and of the mystery of human life."

Vague spirituality has accompanied such vague jurisprudence. Countless liberal theologians have said we can all stand in a hallway of religion without going into particular rooms—but remove the rooms and the hallway is no longer a hallway, just an empty space. Once beliefs are not important and only actions are real, the reason to act disappears.

In short, radical autonomy has merely left us even more like rolling stones. Happily, the Bible repeatedly shows us how to stop rolling and gain satisfaction: "If you walk in my statutes and observe my commandments and do them . . . you shall eat your bread to the full and dwell in your land securely. I will give peace in the land, and you shall lie down, and none shall make you afraid. " (Leviticus 26:3, 5–6).

Ancient Israel had such peace only briefly—and taught us in the process that long-term peace comes only with Christ. And the alternative? Lack of satisfaction, but something even worse: "If your soul abhors my rules . . . I will visit you with panic . . . I will set my face against you" (vv. 15–17).

A Passover Lesson

Two views currently clash about the meaning of American citizenship and how to teach students about it. Some view the US as a uniquely diverse society founded upon the idea of freedom. Others scoff and see the history of America, like that of most other countries, as one of oppression and patriotic gore.

Is America different from other countries? If so, why? Those questions are a little like the question that the youngest child at the table is supposed to ask during the Passover meals that many Jews will eat next week: "Why is this night different from all other nights?"

The Passover Haggadah (order of service) then speaks of "four sons" who have varying reactions to the evening's celebration of deliverance from Egyptian slavery. One is the wicked son, who asks his father, "What is this service to you?" That might seem like a quest for meaning, but the use of "you" means that the wicked son is taking up the posture of an observer who feels superior to those who retain quaint understandings.

Lots of wicked sons teach history in American colleges and schools now. They see America as a land-grabber along with every empire in history. They ignore Colin Powell's true statement about the land the US grabbed in World Wars I and II: just enough to bury our dead. They scream about hypocrisy and lies in Iraq rather than human weakness and mistakes.

Some of these wicked sons are truly wicked. Others have ingested materialist emphases that reduce or even eliminate human choice from history. The Great Man (or great person) teachings of Christmases past sometimes treated men as angels, but many courses now treat humans as either robots or rats.

Another of the four sons in the Haggadah is the wise son, who already knows the story of deliverance. He is like American wise sons who know that our country truly is exceptional. They know we are sinful and fallen, so we've fallen into slavery and have mixed motives about even noble ventures. Overall, though, they see America as a sweet land of liberty.

The tension in the Haggadah account is that the wise son impatiently asks the father to give the story's moral before he's even narrated it in an understandable way. That's the problem in much of our history teaching today. Today, even young children are supposed to develop "critical thinking" about historical problems instead of learning stories of America's patriots. They are taught to see George Washington only as a slaveowner, not as a brave man who staked his life and fortune on the triumph of an idea.

The dad during the Passover seder is supposed to be patient for the sake of his two other sons, one who is "simple" and one who does not know enough to ask a question. In both cases the father is supposed to personalize the story of deliverance by explaining that God delivered "us" or "me" from slavery. The sons cannot understand the intellectual debate, but they can grasp the story and the importance of taking it to heart.

That's what we should do in our history teaching. Polls show that students don't know basic facts, but the problem is deeper than that. Wicked sons teach materialist doctrines. Some wise sons don't teach the tales that help students to love America's past and work optimistically for its future.

Teachers can do better by telling stories about America from a romantic realist perspective. Students need to understand both what happened and why people were excited about those events. Neither a "just the facts" approach or a "just the opinions" approach is sufficient. Students need to appreciate the romance.

Homeschooling parents, using biographies from Greenleaf Press and others that tell of bravery and ideals (none followed perfectly), have often done better than the history pros. For older students, teachers should throw away standard textbooks and instead use popular biographies and histories by writers such as David McCullough, Nathaniel Philbrick (Mayflower), Stephen Ambrose, and others. Neither wickedness nor impatient wisdom will do. Sometimes we have to respect the simple. (2008)

Who's the Invader?

The emergence of religion as an issue in this presidential campaign reminds me of a story about a camping trip taken by fictional characters Sherlock Holmes and Dr. Watson. They go to sleep and wake up soon after dawn. Holmes asks, "Dr. Watson, what do you see?" Watson replies, "I see the sun rising in the east and mountains off to the west. What a wonderful day to be alive!" Holmes responds, "You fool, while we were sleeping someone stole our tent."

If you've read Arthur Conan Doyle's stories you know that Watson doesn't get much respect—but Watson had the better of that conversation. Yes, tents are useful for keeping out rain, flies, snakes, and other critters. But on some mornings, if they block our view of glorious horizons, we're better off without them. (My best nights out, when young, were tentless.) And if putting up a tent means that candidates can't talk about the truly important things in life, open air is certainly better.

Some reporters are writing about the Lieberman and Bush expressions of belief in God as if this were the first time in generations of presidential politics that campaigners went tentless. That shows how short journalistic memories are. Ronald Reagan, for example, talked about God a lot: One study of Reagan speeches in 1983 showed one-tenth of all his prepared remarks to be religious in nature—and most remarkable was not the quantity but the lack of defensiveness.

Some Christian academics look down on Reagan, but they typically mention God only rarely in their work, and are apologetic whenever they do. Reagan never apologized. That's in part because he had a better sense than most of what rendering unto Caesar means. He put it this way during a speech in 1984: "There is much talk in this country now of religion interfering with politics. Actually, it is the other way around. Politics . . . has moved across the barrier between church and state."

This is a critical understanding. It makes no sense to those for whom everything is political. For the proponents of bigger government, rendering unto Caesar what is Caesar's means giving government total sway. But even if we accept that non-constitutional notion of a "wall of separation" between church and state, the important question is where that wall should be situated.

In the Reagan understanding, the Supreme Court's legalization of abortion on demand is an example of national politics invading religion, because it takes away the ability of people in their local communities to defend agreed-upon standards of right and wrong. When local laws require parental consent to ear-piercing but judges declare parental consent to abortion a violation of supposed constitutional rights, national politics once again invades religion.

Prohibition of voluntary prayer in public schools represents yet another invasion, because what goes on in public schools should represent the consensus of local parents (the overwhelming majority of whom want prayer) rather than distant judges. The same logic applies concerning weakening of laws against pornography: Since we are citizens and not subjects, neighbors who can agree on community standards should have the right to keep vile materials out of neighborhood stores.

Some might argue that the cases I've cited involve questions of morality rather than religion, but here I've learned from a columnist of the religious left, Garry Wills. He wrote recently about student responses to three questions: Should church and state be separate? (They said yes.) Should religion and politics be separate? (Yes again.) Should morality and politics be separate? (They said no.) But since most Americans base views of morality on religion, that last answer essentially says that religion and politics should not be separate—and if they are not, then any wall of separation between church and state is porous indeed.

All this means we should go beyond bumper sticker thinking on this subject. The Anti-Defamation League is objecting to the discussion of religion in this year's campaign. "We believe there is a point at which an emphasis on religion in a political campaign becomes inappropriate and even unsettling in a religiously diverse society such as ours," an ADL letter said. But what is that point?

My suggestion to the ADL: the point is where candidates suggest that a particular denomination should be given special privileges, because that is what the first amendment was designed to preclude. Short of that, we're all better off if we can see sunrise in the east and mountains in the west, instead of fearfully pulling down the flaps on our tent. (2000)

Better Hour or Bewitching Hour?

During February, Black History Month, PBS stations around the country have been showing *The Better Hour*, an excellent documentary about William Wilberforce, the great British anti-slavery reformer. The documentary is part of a Better Hour project that includes local gatherings and an essay contest for high school students.

As that documentary is making black (and white) history come alive, another reformer, Barack Obama, is making history in his race against Hillary Clinton for the Democratic presidential nomination. He is also turning on many young evangelicals turned off by politics, in part because, like Wilberforce, he speaks smoothly and doesn't rage at opponents.

Wilberforce, though, stood for more than style. He explained precisely and concretely his abolitionist objective. Obama, though, has not been precise. He speaks of "change," but change can affirm life or can affirm more death, both in the womb and in cities that could be destroyed by nuclear terrorism.

Frankly, I'm tired of conservative talk show rhetoric, so Obama's "Yes We Can!" has an emotional appeal. But can what? Can bridge ideological divides? The non-partisan *National Journal* rates Obama the most liberal member of the Senate. Reduce the amount of lobbying? The only way to do that is to reduce the amount of money Washington controls. (If you build a centralized government, lobbyists will come.)

Obama's talents are obvious: He's a great upgrade over Al Gore and John Kerry! But aren't we to love God with all our heart, soul, mind and strength? Obama does well with hearts, but what about minds?

Obama so far has not agreed to be interviewed by *World*, maybe because we would not be content with the soft questioning he generally receives. He speaks of finding bipartisan solutions to our stickiest problems, but I have yet to hear of any specific solutions he offers that would receive the support of most Republicans as well as most Democrats.

In the absence of the specificity that Wilberforce brought to questions, Obama supporters seem to be part of not "the better hour" (that was poet William Cowper's description of Wilberforce time) but a bewitching hour. The occasional disease of democracy is the tendency for huge numbers of people to put on the back of a charismatic candidate the sum of all their hopes and fears.

These episodes rarely last longer than a year, but during that time much damage can be done. Wilberforce himself complained of those who "either overlook or deny the corruption and weakness of human nature. They . . . speak of man as a being who is naturally pure." Those who think of any politician as pure will inevitably be disappointed.

Obama gets lots of style points, but the question to put to his supporters is: Tell us about the specific Obama policies you think would make things better in America. Give us whatever evidence you have that these policies would succeed. Tell us what his proposals would cost. Tell us, based on the evidence of the past fifty years, how his ideas would improve education and help the poor.

Many people see Obama as the second coming of John F. Kennedy—but Kennedy was a John McCain on foreign policy. He orated in his inaugural address "that we shall pay any price, bear any burden, meet any hardship, support any friend, oppose any foe, in order to assure the survival and the success of liberty." How will a precipitous American retreat from the Middle East make more likely the success of liberty in Iraq?

Kennedy asked Americans to remember that "civility is not a sign of weakness, and sincerity is always subject to proof." Obama's calls for civility deserve praise and emulation, but we need some proof of sincerity in his eloquent calls to bring America together.

The tiniest of markers would be for him to renounce his opposition to last year's Supreme Court upholding of a partial-birth abortion ban. The vast majority of Americans disapprove of that particularly barbaric practice of smashing the skull of a baby during the process of birth. If Obama can't disappoint his pro-abortion backers with even a small gesture, how can we expect him to do anything larger? (2008)

Titanic Futility

On April 15, 1912, the *Titanic* sank. The following year a Constitutional amendment made possible the graduated income tax, and Congress set a top rate of seven percent on incomes above $11 million (in 2012 dollars).

At first taxes were due in March, but in 1955 the due date moved to April 15—apparently for bureaucratic convenience, and not to equate the ship of state with another vessel once thought unsinkable. Titanic arrogance caused 1,517 deaths in 1912. A century later the Obama administration is taking us full speed ahead toward an iceberg of debt.

One strange aspect of the *Titanic*'s sinking: Morgan Robertson, fourteen years before the great disaster, wrote *Futility*, a novel about the sinking of another enormous Atlantic liner. Robertson's fictional ship had almost the same length and tonnage as the *Titanic*, with a high-society first-class passenger list and an insufficient number of lifeboats. Robertson had his ship striking an iceberg on a cold April night and sinking. The title of his fictional ship: the *Titan*.

No one, to my knowledge, has written a novel so prescient concerning our current, slow-motion economic disaster. Some say Ayn Rand did that with *Atlas Shrugged*, but she missed the connection between a biblical worldview and American economic success, and had her hero at book's close making not the sign of the cross but (literally) the sign of the dollar. Her new economic order would have been built on sand.

Nor have the analyses I've seen of the crash of 2008 gotten causality right. Sure, politicians pressured bureaucrats who pressured bankers to loan money to people unlikely to pay it back. Sure, greed in high places and low played a big role. But I think the novel to describe how we've come to our present pass should have an historic name: Futility.

Here's the plot of a new Futility: We used to have a virtuous cycle in Western culture. Parents worked hard to provide for their children. When the parents could no longer work, the children provided for them. That was social security through the centuries.

Given the vagaries of life it wasn't always secure, but in general it worked—and when it did not, extended families, churches, and charitable ministries came alongside widows and orphans.

A new Futility would show twentieth-century government replacing children as the primary provider for those aged and needy. The change liberated elderly folks who were free to move away from their children, and often did. Florida or Arizona grew, but intergenerational contact tragically decreased. Another unanticipated effect: With Social Security, children became financially optional.

That change does not alter the goals of Christians and others who know the true value of children. Bible-believers give up some liberty— children restrict mobility and require responsibility—because we trust God when He says children are a blessing. Our chief purpose in life is to glorify God and enjoy Him forever (which begins right now), and children help us do both: Gifts from God, they bring parents joy.

That change does affect materialists. Some who could have children do not. Others stop at one. Economists could point out that this is a bad bargain: Yes, children are temporarily a money pit, but they are also a great incentive to work. Without that incentive many people work less and depend on the state to bail them out. Children are also an economic blessing to society as they grow and become creators.

More important are psychological consequences of the change: Without an emphasis on work and family, many lack purpose. Some fill up the creeping days and weeks with experiences of different kinds, such as seeing new places and sexually seeking new people. Those who lose sight of eternity define a good life by consumption on earth— whoever gets the most toys wins—rather than preparation for heaven and the training of a new generation.

More important still are social consequences: We replace the virtuous cycle with a downward spiral. Fewer children means fewer workers to support the elderly. When some societies bring in more immigrants to do the work that the never-born members of the next generation would otherwise have done, additional tensions arise.

The spiritual consequences are the greatest. Overall, while politicians unveil plans to save Social Security, Medicare, and other programs, we should recognize that without cultural revival those plans should be stamped: Futility. (2012)

Mascots and Manipulators

The Obama administration on May 13, 2016, directed public schools to allow students to use the bathroom of their choice. Withholding of federal funds could be the prod for schools that don't fall in line. How might Christians think through the transgender issue?

A generation ago some conservatives sneered at "welfare queens" and some liberals made them all heroines. Both generalizations were wrong. A similar problem is evident today in discussion of the much smaller minority known as "transgendered." To some conservatives they are perverts, and that's the end of the discussion. To some liberals they are nature's nobility. A Christian perspective is different from both.

Genesis 1:27 states, "So God created man in his own image, in the image of God he created him; male and female he created them." In the next chapter Adam looks at Eve and says "Bone of my bones, flesh of my flesh." Chapter 2 ends, "Therefore a man shall leave his father and his mother and hold fast to his wife, and they shall become one flesh. And the man and his wife were both naked and were not ashamed." That's it. Everything's great. That's the end of the Bible, right?

Not exactly. Chapter 3 describes the Fall and its terrible consequences: "Cursed is the ground . . . pain . . . sweat. . . . You are dust, and to dust you shall return." Physical disease. Psychological disease. Things aren't right. In looking at anyone, including ourselves, we need to keep in mind both Genesis 1–2 and Genesis 3: We are all made in God's image. We are all sinners. For a small number of humans, one after-effect of Genesis 3 is gender dysphoria, a profound state of depression about one's God-given sex, either male or female.

To grasp that particular effect of original sin, visit the askgender subreddit of Reddit, which with 83 billion page views last year is one of the most-visited US websites. One afternoon's comments included this one: "I've been crying all morning. A friend posted a candid picture of me and all I see is the horrible man I can't escape. . . . This is never ever going away even after years and years of hormones. I want to die . . . why can't I just disappear?"

And this comment: "I feel absolutely like I am a woman stuck in a man's body, and I spend a lot of time thinking and reading about transitioning. I occasionally have these insidious doubts. . . . I've had anxiety since childhood and struggled with depression through my teen years. . . . What if these thoughts of being trans are just me trying to escape from these problems?. . . . Maybe I just want a fresh start, and this is the most extreme way of getting that?"

And this comment: "I want to look like a girl. I never could. My body's an inverted triangle shape . . . My feet are size 12 . . . People say 'suicide is never the answer', but I need to know WHY it's not the answer. Because as far as I can see, it is. That, or I get some bolt of inspiration from God . . . I pray every night. I don't even know who to or what for. Because I need something to change."

Should the rest of us who aren't mixed up in this particular way (we're all mixed up in some way) be trans-despising or trans-phobic? No: The joys God designed in making us male and female, and letting us unite in marriage, are so great that we should be sad regarding anyone who doesn't have them. Our battle is not with depressed transgenders but with those who make them "mascots"—to use Thomas Sowell's expression about liberal use of poor people—and put them on display. (Sowell: "The problem with being a mascot is that you are a symbol of someone else's significance or virtue. The actual well-being of a mascot is not the point.")

Here's one comment I ran across on Reddit last year: "I'm transgender. . . . Countless trans people tell me and others . . . the only reason we feel badly about ourselves is because of how cis people judge us. I knew my body was screwed up before I even knew what the term cis meant. . . . Whenever I go to support groups or LGBT events, I'm always lumped in with people who hate non-trans people, want to break down all of the oppressive systems around them, and frankly just want to be seen. The thing is, I don't want to be seen. I don't want to be a femme genderqueer trans boi. I just wanna be a normal guy."

Since it's now a legal requirement in New York City to address a person with the pronoun and title the person wants, here are two more relevant Reddit comments: "I'm trans . . . and I have never met anyone who says . . . 'fight the cistem' or insists upon flavour of the month makey-upey pronouns, or tells anyone else the only reason we feel bad about our bodies is cis people." And, "I knew a genderqueer couple that required you use rotating pronouns for them. (xe, she, he, xis, his, her) I just said 'they' or didn't talk to them. . . . Most trans people just want to live . . . and not turn everything into a battle."

When Christians enter into bathroom-use debates, we should distinguish between those building careers as transgender activists by deliberately rebelling against God's order, and those who resent mascot treatment and merely want to find a way to minimize their soul-tearing misery. Strugglers should be shown the love of Christ. Agitators for whom "equality" is not an end-state but an industry—and, sadly, perhaps even a religion—also need compassion, in the form of truth delivered in love.

All of them, like all of us, need God, and we reduce the possibility of their finding Him if we react to the "We win, you lose" demands of media-designated spokespeople merely by shouting back, "No—we win, you lose." (2016)

Individual Responses

Harmed by CNN blowhards who politicized hurricane reporting and largely neglected the work of Christian volunteers and others, the American image around the world took a post-Katrina nosedive. "I am absolutely disgusted," said Sajeewa Chinthaka of Sri Lanka. "After the tsunami our people, even the ones who lost everything, wanted to help the others who were suffering."

The problem, some said, was "American individualism," with folks acting selfishly. Hmmm. That can be a problem among those who worship only the trinity of "me, myself, and I," but tens of thousands of Americans individuals eagerly responded to the crisis without waiting for governmental or collective directive.

Before expressing disgust with America, please spend a couple of hours reading through Internet postings like this one: "We are a family of five. . . . We have a very small room with a bed and two small dressers that we will offer to you so that you can get back on your feet. You will be welcome at our family table and we'll help you in any way you need, getting a job, reaching family, getting clothes, and whatever else. We don't have much money after the bills are paid, but we'll happily share whatever we can. We don't expect you to pay us, and we won't expect you to leave quickly. It takes time to rebuild and we'll give you that time."

The apostle Paul wrote about how many different parts of the body contribute to its functioning, and that's true for a country responding to charity as it is for a church: "I am a licensed bus driver willing to go south to haul those folks out. . . . I am a house painter. . . . I am fully licensed, have a truck with all equipment and chemicals, and am willing to go down and help out with any pest control problems. . . . I'm a building and roofing contractor from upstate New York who will donate my expertise and labor. . . . I am background-screened and fingerprinted for childcare, willing to take in a few kids or a small family. . . . I speak fluent Spanish and will contact anyone for anybody."

Medical personnel were volunteering: "I'm a board-certified orthopedic surgeon who is willing to help in a medical capacity. . . . I am a nurse from Cleveland. . . . I am a fully-licensed general surgery chief resident willing to help immediately. . . . I am a CPR-certified healthcare provider." Some specialists were willing to be generalists: "Hi, I'm a registered nurse, my boyfriend is a union electrician. Even if you couldn't use us in our professions we would be willing to provide any assistance necessary."

Many people offered housing: "Can't get out there myself, but we have a dry, clean living room with space for a small family and their pets. . . . We only have our hearts and our home to offer, but our home is comfortable and dry! . . . I am a single mother with a small baby at home. I have an extra room and can house a single parent and/or children. It's not a lot of space but I can help with meals, clothing, employment, and schooling. . . . We are licensed, loving foster parents who would be honored to take in a baby/toddler/young child—short or long term."

Many people without special training or available space just offered themselves: "I was down at ground zero after 9/11 and can help with any manual labor, rebuilding, medical help, search and rescue, and anything else under the sun. . . . I cannot offer my apartment for shelter at this time because I have no power/water, and I cannot offer money because I have very little, but I am very able to help out physically. . . . I have two husky chainsaws, transportation, and complete camping and cooking gear. No pay required, just a destination and a person who truly needs help."

Television viewers abroad may have seen images of helplessness, but many would-be volunteers showed a can-do spirit: "I can run heavy equipment or operate off-road vehicles and a variety of boats in highly variable and adverse conditions. I have extensive experience in the coastal marshes and swamps of south LA and MS and have construction, oilfield, and welding experience. I can also cook. I'll do anything to help and I can bring some supplies." And many who couldn't provide much material aid helped in another crucial way: "God bless you all. I continue to pray." (2005)

SECTION THREE:
INSTITUTIONS

This section's columns examine the limitations of purported panaceas such as campaign spending limits, more hours of volunteering, and more dollars in college funds. Partisan solutions are partial at most and often designed to make the world safe for hypocrisy: some Democrats succeed by wrapping the language of compassion around socialist ideas, and some Republicans win by wrapping biblical references around Social Darwinist ideas.

Christians should be Post-resurrection Peters regarding faith in God, but Doubting Thomases regarding faith in man's organizations—which means we should poke fingers in their sides. For example, big institutions such as The University of Texas at Austin, where I was a professor for twenty-five years, do not provide the mentoring that leads to real education. Grade inflation hinders useful self-evaluation. Many undergraduates learn to do minimally satisfactory work in many areas rather than exceptional work in one.

I also argue that Christians need to examine corruption and not pretend that everything is fine. When Paul tells us in Philippians 4:8 to think about what's good, he could not have meant that we are never to think of what is dishonorable, unjust, and worthy of condemnation, or else he could not have carried out his evangelical work amid a pagan society.

Amoral, Moralistic, and Biblical Reviewing

Now that *Saving Private Ryan* is readily available at video stores, it's time to revisit a firefight sparked by *World*'s review of the film (Aug. 8, 1998) when it was playing in theaters. Many letters that we printed took *World* to task for praising a film that contained graphic violence and bad language, and not warning readers about the latter.

As is our custom, we did not print our response to the criticism. My belief is that after we've taken our shot readers should freely take theirs, without having to worry about any sarcastic put-downs. But now that more of our readers are seeing the film for themselves, let's deal with some fundamental issues.

World's movie and television reviews assume that Christians should not live in a cultural ghetto and should develop points of contact with the non-Christians who surround us. Our models here are Daniel and Paul, both of whom displayed knowledge of the pagan poetry and theology that surrounded them. We respect Christians who want to isolate themselves from worldliness, but *World*'s primary calling is to cover the world, not the church. We also see nothing wrong with the pleasure that watching a good movie or show provides.

Within that context, our reviews have three functions. They should help our readers decide whether to see something that sounds appealing. They should give readers some sense of the pictures that are dancing through the heads of our fellow citizens. They should summarize and biblically critique the worldviews of our key cultural teachers.

The triple task makes the reviewer's job hard. He has to be both a regent (standing in for readers, as their eyes and ears) and a teacher. He needs the discernment to bring out theological implications and the light-heartedness to enjoy movies that aren't theological treatises. He needs the ability to look at what other people see but then see it more deeply through adept use of a biblical lens.

Along with the triple task, a *World* reviewer needs to understand the triple distinction—amoral, moralistic, and biblical—that underlies our general reporting philosophy. Many reviewers today are amoral, worshiping sensation for sensation's sake, reveling in slow-motion murder and fast-talking obscenity, not even paying attention to whether films and programs glorify evil.

Some moralistic reviewers appropriately attack the amoral but then push smiley-faced films that preach faith in man's natural goodness. These reviewers criticize amoral destruction but don't note how the subtle sapping of moralism can be even more effective in keeping us from seeing our need for God's grace. They roll over for smarmy products designated as "uplifting"—but uplift apart from Christ is idolatry.

Biblical reviewers, however, look for films and programs that help us to comprehend evil and the need to fight it. They praise unblinking eyes that take in man's depravity when those eyes are controlled by a biblically-directed brain that shows sin's consequences. They know that Christianity is not a nice religion: Just as priests used hyssop to spray the blood of sacrifices on the people in Moses's time, so Christ had to shed His blood, not just preach, to free us from sin. Those who follow Him should not hide from hard realities either in life or on film.

Discussion of hard realities brings us back to *Saving Private Ryan*, which I've now watched on video after missing it in the movie theaters. On the to-see-or-not-to-see question, we clearly failed by not telling readers of the bad (although historically accurate) language. On the describe-the-hit question, we did a good job of succinctly summarizing the D-Day film's power.

But it's the theology suggested at the end of the film that I find most intriguing. One dying soldier's last words to the man whose life he and others saved, at great cost, are "Earn this. Earn it." Then we fast-forward half a century: the man who was saved, now old, is in a cemetery, hobbling to a cross that commemorates his savior. The old man fights back tears to say, "I lived my life the best I could. I hope that was enough." But has he "earned it"? He turns to his wife and pleads, "Tell me I'm a good man." His wife says, "you are"—and there are his children and grandchildren behind him.

The gospel according to director Stephen Spielberg is evident here, as it was in *Schindler's List*. We can pay for the life that's been given us by our good works—although we're never sure if we've done enough. And yet, at the end of *Saving Private Ryan* a shadow lurks: We cannot shake the mystery of grace offered by a man dying for us. Maybe some of us can discuss with non-Christian moviegoers how Christianity alone brings into harmonious tension the earning and the gift. (1999)

The Dream Factory

Why have movie and television reviews at all? Why review programs or films that are not child-friendly? Why not just review evangelical films specifically made for Christian audiences? Three reasons:

1. God's common grace does allow some good secular productions to come into existence, and most *World* readers like to know about them.

2. Hollywood is still America's dream factory: just as Daniel had to understand Babylonian culture in order to interact effectively with the rulers around him, so we must know the dreams that have become central to ours.

3. The Christian cultural separatist dream is dead. Walk into any evangelical church and it is likely that most of the teens there have watched *Friends* and other hit shows; we need to know how to react.

Our task at *World*, then, must be to review major media products, or else we are not being true to the mission statement printed each week on page four. The reviewer's job is difficult, though, because it involves not only service as the eyes and ears of our readers, but teaching discernment as well. It is always important to warn readers about violence, sexual suggestiveness, and profanity, but merely totaling up manifestations of sin is a task for an accountant, not a trainer.

Yes, Hollywood's fixation on sex must be fought, but at the same time we should note the deeper danger: Consumers of popular culture, including Christians, are often subtly conditioned to oppose transcendental reality and objective virtue.

Yes, be careful little children what you see, but what's more shattering than an occasional shoot-out is the common presentation of a world without religion, one in which noble thoughts are rarely uttered during prime time and even tough-guy protagonists who pretend to be men of steel are morally sad sacks of straw.

We should not attempt to be holier than God by declaring that evidence of man's depravity, which the Scriptures emphasize so emphatically, is off-limits for Christians today. That's why during the past year our film reviewer gave two cheers to riveting but uncomfortable movies like *Braveheart* and *Rob Roy*.

We will not duck such difficult encounters, but we long to praise films and programs that show how spectacular the unspectacular can be. A fine film from the '80s, *Tender Mercies*, quietly showed the sweetness of small moments, and we are celebrating this year the fiftieth anniversary of a movie that did that best of all: Director Frank Capra's *It's a Wonderful Life* (1946) delightfully depicts a type of born-again experience, and also illustrates the perseverance in doing good that Christians are to have.

After all, the hero of that movie, played by Jimmy Stewart, could have done great things by worldly standards. He could have moved to the big city. He could have joined the big bank at a greatly increased salary—yet he sticks with his tiny outfit that merely gives hard-working poor folks the opportunity to own their own homes. The film resonates with me every time I visit a good but struggling inner city Christian poverty-fighting group and contrast it with well-funded government welfare organizations.

How many of this year's movies will be remembered fifty years from now? How many are remembered fifty days after release? Frank Capra had not only genius, but a "sense of responsibility," according to novelist Graham Greene, "a kinship with his audience, a sense of common life, a morality."

Capra's films, including *Mr. Smith Goes to Washington* and *Meet John Doe*, move well not just because he had good intentions. Since, in Capra's words, "crowd reactions are precisely what the film was made for in the first place," he taped preview showings and, listening to the tapes, noted that "when the film was interest-grabbing the audience was silent, hushed. Where it was dull or long, I heard coughs, shufflings, rattlings of peanut bags." Capra then re-edited the film to maximize interest.

Capra made movies move, and that's a feature some deeply moral films and programs lack. What's missing from most of today's bad entertainment products is a morality that overarches the minute to minute and can last a lifetime. What's missing from some films praised by evangelical reviewers for their decency is enough cough-silencing action.

Morality and movement: At *World*, we're constantly looking for products that combine the two. When we find something good, we will tell you about it in our pages. We will also critique the bad, so you can tell others how far short of true good it falls. (1998)

Marriage—Thanking God for a Great Gift

The DOMA (Defense of Marriage Act) debate discussed in our cover story should not have to take place. It should be part of a before-dinner prayer, like "Thank you, God, for this food, for this day, and for marriage." From the time my children were little we've generally kept grace before meals succinct and highly specific; after dinner is the time for discussion of not-so-obvious prayer needs. So how did something so basic as marriage move from before dinner to after dinner?

It's easy to blame gay politics and pandering politicians, especially since they deserve blame. Nothing in what follows should be taken as criticism of DOMA: Congress should pass it. But let's acknowledge a difficult truth: heterosexual adultery creates havoc in more families and churches than homosexuality does, and churches rarely fight this #1 culprit by preaching, effective shepherding, or use of church discipline.

Why? For many pastors, the task is too daunting. They would have to battle the worldview—call it Playboyism—that has the dominant advertising space throughout much of American culture. Movies, ads, and talk shows all suggest to men especially that either being single or acting that way offers varieties of physical pleasure and a sense of psychological conquest. Surveys show the reality is very different, and just what we would expect from reading the Bible: married sex beats unmarried sex in both quality and quantity. But that's not what a Martian coming to earth and viewing the lies of both popular and high culture would suspect.

Lies, once believed, have consequences. Promiscuous singles even in their twenties have problems, but as young bodies become old and loneliness swamps lust, the abc's of alienation, brokenness, and confusion become even more evident. Sometimes, though, reality doesn't sink in until people are forty or even fifty, and by then decades are gone and cannot be replaced. The situation is better for people who resist Playboyism enough to get married—but even after that temptations sink many ships, as the divorce rate suggests.

When I was purportedly pursuing higher education, I wasn't a Christian. I bought what James Bond movies and a host of others were teaching even then: the good life is sleeping with many different women. Since becoming a Christian a quarter-century ago I've often thanked God that He did not make me handsome or rich. If He had, I would have sinned sexually more than I did, because I had to work very hard for opportunities. What if instead of getting married I had bought the lie? What if at age fifty-one I did not have a wife with whom I have shared a quarter-century of faithful love, and four sons of whom I am very proud? Assuming I had not died of or been debilitated by some disease, I would still be among the saddest of men.

Playboyism leads not only to personal tragedies but to enormous public effects. When a man and a woman marry, poverty takes a hit: the *Journal of Marriage and the Family* reports that never married mothers are ten times more likely to be on welfare than married mothers. When a man and a woman stay married and faithful to each other, sexual promiscuity drops not only for their generation but the next: the National Health and Social Life Survey found that teens whose parents remain married are much more likely to abstain from sex and avoid problems that include out-of-wedlock pregnancy.

Let me reiterate that being anti-Playboy should not be confused with being anti-pleasure. A famous Christian declaration from the 1640s, the Westminster Confession of Faith, includes some Q and A. The most famous question is this one: What is the chief end of man?—end meaning purpose. The answer goes, "To glorify God and enjoy Him forever." Forever begins right now, and God has given us numerous ways to enjoy Him, including being in bed with the person to whom you're married.

All through this month of June, the biggest wedding month of the years, we should thank God for marriage in before-dinner prayers. After dinner, depending on the age of our children, we should discuss how marriage is under attack from various directions. We should pray for the legislative defense of marriage but even more for its cultural defense, because if we forsake the first institution God established for the creatures made in His own image, what will stop us from relinquishing every one of His kind provisions? (2002)

Old Blacklisting and New

"**B**lacklisting." A senior in the journalism history course I teach at the University of Texas did not know who U. S. Grant was, but she knew all about the dreaded "McCarthy era," that time in those dismal 1950s when sweet, kind Hollywood screenwriters on the left had trouble getting jobs.

That's typical. Many of the students who graduated from major universities this month have a distorted view of the past. Most have sat through lectures emphasizing minor episodes designed to teach students about the nastiness of the right or the virtues of the left. Most have no understanding of the role of Christianity in American history.

Even when it comes to "blacklisting," few students learned about Hollywood's discrimination against Christians and conservatives during the 1960s, 1970s, 1980s, and 1990s. They never heard of the Hollywood Stalinist tyranny of the mid-1940s, even though Screen Actors Guild president Ronald Reagan got his political start standing up against it.

One reason few students learned what actually happened is because of the academic blacklisting of Christians and conservatives that occurs today. I was reminded of this recently by a telephone call from David Snodgrass, chairman of the Mass Communication Dept. at Florida Southern University. He was calling because I had supervised the doctoral dissertation of a candidate for a faculty position there, and he wanted my opinion of that gentleman's capabilities.

And then, hesitantly, Prof. Snodgrass asked for something more: "There's, uh, one question that arose concerning [the candidate's] background . . . just a hunch, something that came out of my going through his vita . . . 1977–79, assistant managing editor, *Good News Magazine*."

When I asked what the hunch was about a job from two decades before, Prof. Snodgrass whispered the horrible possibility: Is the candidate a "fundamentalist"? The concern, he hastened to say, was not with religious belief as such, but "We would not want a person who held beliefs that would interfere with his ability to do mainstream scholarship. . . . We are so very, very eager to have someone doing mainstream research and publication. We want someone who will be nationally recognized, who will have stature in the field."

Prof. Snodgrass's caution is logical. Given the bigotry of leading academics and their journals, a fundamentalist (unless he stays in the closet) will be frozen out, and a university's national reputation will not grow. But is such discrimination right? How many universities have informal blacklists against Bible-believing Christians or political conservatives?

I have some personal experience with academic bigotry. During my first year in graduate school as an atheist and a communist, professors at the University of Michigan called me a genius; they were wrong. When I left as a Christian and a conservative, one professor believed I had become a moron; he also was wrong, but he tried to keep me from receiving a PhD, and probably would have succeeded but for the intervention of the one outspokenly conservative professor on campus.

Ever since then I have been very sensitive to ideological bias in grading: I have been teaching at the University of Texas since 1983, and in all that time no student, to my knowledge, has ever accused me of such unfairness. But, from what students have told me and shown me concerning other courses, it does appear that such bias occurs elsewhere. This is not to say that I'm a more virtuous grader than others; since I work in hostile territory and know that everything I say or do is examined critically, I would have to play it straight with grades even if my preferences were to push me in a different direction. Such restraints may not exist elsewhere.

We do not know what informal blacklisting does to the academic prospects of Christians and conservatives. I have been blessed with good health, a tough skin, a supportive family and church, and the ability to write fairly quickly. But lots of others who refuse to ignore God in their work never get through the ideological pounding of graduate school, never get a university job, never get tenure.

The culture war going on throughout the United States is becoming ever more vicious in our academic hothouses. Discerning alumni and taxpayers should ask whether the universities they support have a policy, "No fundamentalists allowed." Christian students and professors should not allow themselves to be shut up, slammed down, and forced out without a fight. When they are attacked, they deserve the full support of Christian alumni, taxpayers, and the entire church community. (1997)

Do Not Choose Colleges by Prestige Alone

College students regularly e-mail jokes about their schools' traditional rivals. One southeastern set of "How many does it take to screw in a lightbulb?" digs includes: "At Tennessee it takes only one, but he gets seven credits for it . . . At Ole Miss it takes five. One to change it, and four to find the perfect J. Crew outfit to wear for the occasion . . . At LSU it takes 104. One to screw the darn thing in and 103 to bring the beer . . . At Vanderbilt, it takes two. One to screw it in, and one to say how they did it as well as Ivy Leaguers." And so on.

For many high school seniors and their parents this spring, the choice of colleges is no laughing matter. Some ambitious students ask one main question: "Which college will be best for gaining a good job or an advanced degree following graduation, as well as general prestige that I can lean on throughout life?" For such students, Yale is automatically better than Vanderbilt, Vanderbilt better than Auburn, and Auburn better than just about any Christian college, since only a few of the latter are well respected in law school halls or corporate corridors.

Some wealthy parents are all too willing to pay $120,000 and up for four years of a designer label school. Even though at many lauded institutions faithful Christian students are lonely sheep among wolves, parents who value social cachet will go into debt to provide sons and daughters with a crutch that gives them the opportunity not to use their talents to their fullest.

That's right, a crutch. Students at elite universities can slouch toward graduation and still gain good placements afterward. A student with the same talent at a less prestigious school has to achieve an excellent grade point average and do well on standardized exams to get to the same place. The student with a designer label degree is able to do childish things for a while after graduation and still reenter the fast track. The other student needs to be an adult at age twenty-one. But is that a bad thing? Providentially, the United States is still a country where intelligence and hard work matter, and it's good for students to know that their economic future depends on their efforts.

Many students this spring will kiss their fat envelopes when they receive acceptances from the most prestigious schools. But bright students looking for exposure to top-notch professors should understand the "bait and switch" tendency of leading universities: gain recognition through professorial prestige but assign many teaching duties to graduate students. Deeper questions should be asked: Where is a student most likely to grow spiritually and intellectually? Where is he most likely to find a calling and become well-prepared for it? Where is he most likely to find godly enjoyment of his college years?

Many students, after considering those questions, may head to a Christian college where the gospel has not been watered down and where brains as well as hearts are considered important. At a good Christian college, students will learn to think biblically from professors who teach them to rebel not against the Church but against America's leading religion, secular liberalism. Spiritually-strong students who already have a Christian worldview might decide to accept the challenge of study at a secular university—but they should choose one with a strong chapter of Reformed University Fellowship or some other biblically-tough campus ministry.

Parents sometimes ask questions about curricular matters, but since students often learn more from their peers than from their professors, it's also important to assess student culture and politics. It's hard to stand up against drugs, alcohol abuse, and secular liberal politics if everyone around is indulging. Being a missionary at age eighteen is not for everyone, but with God's grace and a good support system, students can do well, develop deep friendships, and also gain needed toughness as they respond to anti-Christian attacks.

The biggest mistake in college-picking, however, comes in demand-ing bread alone. A woman who searches for a rich suitor is called a gold-digger. The same should be said of a student who selects a college for its designer label. Bright students generally don't need a crutch; they can make it on their own. Christian students specifically should not rely on a crutch; they rest on the cross. The right college for a Christian is not one that will merely strengthen his résumé. It is one that will go the furthest in strengthening heart, soul, and mind. (1999)

Beyond Knee-Jerk Giving

This is the time of year when many college alumni respond to their nagging alma mater by sending a contributions check made out to the institution's general fund. Here's one word of advice: "Don't" (unless you want to support theological and political liberalism).

Oh, a few Christian colleges may be exceptions to that four-letter rule, but even then we should trust, but verify. Skepticism is even more important at major state or secular universities. For two decades I've seen and heard about the harassment that Christian and conservative professors and students often receive. Some students have stood their ground and some professors have carved out niches, but secular liberals contest every inch.

What will happen? Gutsy conservatives like David Horowitz have declared war and are marshalling statistics. Democrats outnumber Republicans nearly 30–1 among anthropologists and sociologists, according to the National Association of Scholars. Surveys of voter registration among humanities and social science professors at twenty universities including Cornell, Stanford, Brown, California-Berkeley, and Colorado showed left/right ratios of anywhere from 8–1 to 28–1. If the surveys were to examine theology rather than politics and ask about faith in Christ, the numbers would be even more skewed.

Will those stats prompt action to increase a diversity of ideas? Most universities are heavily dependent on government funding, and some Republicans are asking why they should continually subsidize their opponents. There'll be demands for fair hiring of ideological minorities (conservatives), but such requirements will be hard to pass or to enforce. The best move would be for state legislatures to create a level playing field in higher education by offering scholarships usable at any college—governmental, private, or religious. That would foster competition rather than conformity in higher education, but we're probably a generation away from such change.

So, for the time being, how can conservative Christians promote alternatives within the belly of the beast? Four suggestions, in rising order of wallet size.

First, instead of writing undesignated checks, direct funds to Christian groups on campus such as Reformed University Fellowship, InterVarsity Christian Fellowship, or Cru. Important questions to ask: Is a group helping students to think Christianly about what arises in their courses? Does a group implicitly tell students not to make waves academically, or does it instruct and honor those who stand up against classroom propaganda?

Second, contribute to the creation and staffing of Christian study centers near campus. Such centers should have fellows and tutors capable of challenging secular conventions, and libraries with books and films that display an alternative, biblical reality.

Third, if you want to contribute directly to a university-sponsored program, find out which professors (if any) are conservative Christians and unafraid to speak out about the issues of the day. Designate donations to support their research, writing, and training of graduate students.

Fourth, if you have lots of money and want to make a big difference, go beyond campus groups, study centers, and individual professors, and work to set up programs within universities. Some moderates and conservatives, with great determination, have already done that at institutions like Princeton, Duke, Brown, Colgate, the U. of Colorado, City University of New York, the U. of Nebraska-Omaha, and the U. of Alaska.

Some of these programs are little more than beachheads. Some emphasize good free market principles but not other biblical values. Others emphasize natural law in an appealing way, but don't examine Scripture as deeply as they should. Those efforts are helpful, and Christians participate in some of them, but to my knowledge no major state or secular university has a program designed to advance Christian understanding in the campus marketplace, even though Islamic centers abound.

In some ways the lack of evangelical-led programs reflects the tiny number of outspoken evangelicals within the humanities and social sciences faculties at major universities. In some ways that paucity also reflects a failure of vision among major donors, and the difficulty of getting past college deans who hate Christ.

It's important to remember, though, that many academic officials who have turned their backs on God now serve Mammon, and cannot help salivating at the sight of a check waved in front off them. If funding emerges, breakthroughs will come. (2005)

Education and Welfare

Good news from *The New York Times*! The newspaper of record noted earlier this month, "Students' Test Scores Show Slow but Steady Gains at Nation's Schools." It seems that 60 percent of American fourth-graders showed a minimal reading competence! If that's not cause for celebration, try this: 78 percent of thirteen-year-olds can add, subtract, multiply, and divide! That's up from 75 percent in 1990!

Let's get real, press propagandists. The *Times* pretends that the public school system is not an utter failure. *Newsweek* in a cover story exults about "Generation G," young high-tech Americans traveling throughout the globe. Meanwhile, millions of children are left behind, with so little knowledge of reading, writing, and arithmetic that they can't even qualify for the low-tech jobs that remain.

In your own community, dear reader, you may also be encountering educational happytalk. The threat of home schools and private schools was supposed to make the government schools do better; it has certainly made them hire more public relations staffers. In my own city of Austin, for example, the press releases hit the front page when eleven schools pulled themselves off the low-performing list and became "acceptable." That sounds great: but, "acceptable" only means that at least 35 percent of the students passed the Texas Assessment of Academic Skills test.

Is a 35 percent success rate good news? Is it good news when even that figure is achieved only with some caveats and quid pro quos, as the genie in Aladdin might say. The newspaper reports did not explain that the TAAS test itself has a reputation as a dumbed-down exam.

And it took some digging to find out that a school showing "significant improvement" may be rated acceptable even if it does not achieve that stupendous success rate of 35 percent.

Is your local school district fudging its failure the same way? Has it also lowered its expectations so far that it regards a thirty-five percent pass rate as acceptable? Let me see if I can figure out a TAAS-type question: If at least 35 percent pass, doesn't that mean that up to 65 percent fail? And in that case, how can anyone who is not cruel consider those schools "acceptable"? How can anyone in good conscience send so many children from these schools out into the world with so little preparation?

Maybe guilt about continued educational failure is the reason why so many governmental officials are so eager to return us to the failed welfare system. Maybe they see no alternative to bringing back not the New Deal (which emphasized work) but the Bad Deal for millions of Americans, a Bad Deal that goes like this: Don't complain about the poor education you receive. Give up your hopes to break out of poverty. And we, in turn, will keep you on the welfare rolls indefinitely, exempt from work "requirements."

To get a good job, get a good education. To go on welfare, be one of the many who lose out at an "acceptable" school. Lying to kids by telling them their bad schools are acceptable really does make me mad. Two studies several years ago showed that 60–67 percent of inner city teen females believed they would not be any worse off if they became pregnant. Most of those very young women, in other words, saw welfare support as a given, and did not see economic advance likely, so there was no reason not to become a single parent and remain poor, but with a child to love. Most of them probably went to acceptable schools.

Welfare reform was designed to change the message, but now the Bad Deal is back. And many inner city males, poorly educated in our "acceptable" schools, will continue to receive an equally tragic message: You're not needed economically. Uncle Sam will move in with your woman, so get lost, or pick up a Go to Jail card.

This is bleak but true, I fear—and imposing a nationwide testing system is likely only to make things worse. There is only one kind of good news that is believable here, and it is the good news of Jesus

Christ. Our central educational question should be: How will more children, poor as well as affluent, have access to schools that transmit the good news that they, and all of us, desperately need?

If we don't come up with a good answer and put it into practice, welcome to a bleak twenty-first century. (1997)

Rolling Back Welfare Reform

It's working—even *The New York Times* realizes that. It's working—and Congressional liberals, along with some fearful Republicans, are poised to snatch defeat from victory's jaws.

The "it" is welfare reform. Recently a *Times* headline—"In Sink-or-Swim Welfare, Pensacola Staying Afloat"—noted good news. Most former welfare recipients have done fine in the Florida city that three years ago imposed time limits on welfare benefits. (The whole country came along last August, when President Clinton reluctantly signed the Republican bill.)

The *Times*, which vigorously fought serious welfare reform on its editorial page, quoted on its news pages thirty-nine-year-old mother Denis Riley, who refused to work as long as she was receiving a welfare check. Last September her time was up, and liberals predicted doom. But Ms. Riley says, "I went to work a week later. I had to."

She now stocks the buffet at a pizzeria for $5.75 an hour, and calls her ouster from welfare a blessing: "It made me wake up and get my priorities back in order. I'll be honest: I might have leaned on that check a little longer."

Pensacola evidently has many such stories, and many more are developing all across the country. These stories are no surprise: The Bible teaches that we are all fallen human beings who need to be challenged to do the right thing. Any time a false understanding of compassion leads politicians to patronize potentially hard-working adults by offering entitlements, we harm the poor under the guise of doing good.

Welfare reform will work, if we let it. Here's the danger: the *Times* also quoted a welfare mom who is resisting the change. Tatashia Holley, twenty-four, complained that her caseworkers "wanted people to go to McDonald's. I got too much pride for that. I didn't go to school for that stinking paycheck."

The story reported the problems that ensued after Ms. Holley's refusal. She had to move to a dilapidated building. She may have to place her children in foster care. This is sad, but what if welfare officials give in now and say, "Holley, you're right, it is ennobling to be on welfare and demeaning to flip burgers"? One young woman (and eventually millions of others) will lose the opportunity for real change. They and their children will be condemned to life on welfare.

As anyone who works behind a fast food counter knows—I learned it when I was young, one of my sons has learned it this summer—those jobs are great for teaching responsible behavior. If Holley swallowed her false pride and worked hard, she'd be able to move from a beginning job to a better job, and eventually that stinking paycheck would smell pretty sweet.

The *Times* article is important, because it goes against the grain. The tendency of liberal journalists and professors is to highlight the short-term, tear-jerking stories that emerge, and ignore the positive changes.

Already, many of the official welfare experts seem intent on greasing the slide back to Egyptian bondage. One of this year's academic books on welfare, Rebecca Blank's *It Takes a Nation: A New Agenda for Fighting Poverty*, skillfully fights to retain much of the old agenda.

On the other hand, three helpful books have come out over the past eighteen months. I wrote one entitled *Renewing American Compassion*, but overall I like better Michael Tanner's *The End of Welfare*. There's also Susan Mayer's *What Money Can't Buy*, a book that conveys very well the understanding that welfare transfers are not the answer.

Which way will Washington go? So far this summer, the news from the capital is bad. The Senate's Budget Reconciliation Act, if agreed to by the House of Representatives, will increase welfare spending, outlaw meaningful workfare, and eliminate most of the pressure on welfare recipients to work.

Conservatives ordinarily would have no problem just saying no to such retro notions, but the present state of organizational confusion in the House of Representatives gives liberals an opening. Pundits so far are talking about that confusion, highlighted recently by the anti-Gingrich coup, as if its repercussions were merely political. But the retreat from principle, coupled by a loss of party discipline, is not only derailing careers but threatening a rollback of everything conservatives accomplished in 1995 and 1996.

Welfare reform was the crown jewel of what once was called the Republican Revolution. Now, the heist is underway. It is likely to succeed unless Christians and conservatives rally and demand that Congressional leaders get their House in order. (1997)

Volunteering by Itself
Is Morally Neutral

Two weeks ago reporters presented two sides of the story concerning the Clinton/Powell summit on volunteerism. One side, emphasizing Philadelphia's brotherly love, was summit-gung-ho. The other, noting that good vibrations cannot make up for government welfare reductions, was summit-scornful.

The problem, however, is that there was a third side, and it was not heard. Maybe that third position can best be grasped by thinking of the judge late last month who declared cigarettes to be a delivery vehicle for a drug, nicotine. The two sides quoted by summit reporters were arguing about the delivery vehicle: government or volunteers? But the more important question, one that was ignored, concerned the substance being delivered.

That question is critical in poverty-fighting. Historically and in recent times, programs (whether government-run or volunteer-based) that provide entitlement, live by bureaucracy, and attempt to banish God, almost never work. Programs that are challenging, personal, and spiritual, if they are well-managed, do. Overall, smaller organizations tend to do better than larger ones, but changing the delivery vehicle is of little help if the same substance is delivered.

For instance, will wiping graffiti off a wall yield more than a politician's photo opportunity if the attitudes that produced the graffiti in the first place remain unchanged? Will thousands of mentors cut down teen pregnancy rates, if the mentors do not push for abstinence? (The use of contraceptives with a ninety percent success rate will eventually result in pregnancy.)

Substance, substance. It may be a good thing that the state of California will give employees release time to tutor children (although paid volunteering does seem to be a contradiction in terms). But reading levels in California plunged when state edu-crats disregarded phonics, and changing the delivery system for teaching children without changing the substance will not help much.

The summit skipped by questions of substance for three reasons. First was public relations: Applause all around plays better than ideological discussion. But some summit defenders of the welfare mentality were also doing a clever tactical repositioning. They know that most Americans want to help people in poverty who are willing to work hard, but not those who are unwilling. They know that most Americans are ready to insist on the centrality of work, family, and faith, and are unwilling to pay more in taxes to enable the opposite. Therefore, the mission is clear: change part of the delivery system from government to corporate, with companies looking for government favors pressuring their employees to volunteer for neoliberal entitlement programs.

The summit was also substance-less because the few conservatives involved in its planning were willing to bleach out their ideas in the interest of broad acceptability. Conservative welfare reform always has had both the carrot (we will help) and the stick (we'll require you to work). Both parts are necessary, since without real pressure there is often unwillingness to change behavior. The summit narrowed its focus to become all sweetness: mentor the children. But streetwise folks know they cannot help the children without challenging many of the parents to change their ways.

None of these comments is intended to criticize discerning volunteerism. But just as there is nothing holy in faith itself—the key question is always, faith in what?—so there is no redemption in volunteerism itself. Volunteering by itself is morally neutral. A stress on method alone is social madness.

What should discerning volunteers do when the Clinton/Powell photo op crowd arrives? I'm reminded of an old Texas story about a young farm girl out milking the family cow when a stranger approaches and asked to see her mother.

"Momma," the young lady calls out, "there's a man here to see you." The mother looks out the kitchen window and replies, "Haven't I always told you not to talk to strangers? You come in this house right now." The girl protests: "But momma, this man says he is a United States senator." The wise mother replies, "In that case, bring the cow in with you."

When the summiteers come calling, head for cover and bring the cow in too. (1997)

Political Parties

Some of our readers view the clash of political parties as meaningless. Here's a letter from Pete Berglar of St. Louis: "I try not to be a cynic, because God is in control, not Democrats or Republicans. Nevertheless, I find myself agreeing more often than I'd like with the old saw about the two parties: 'there's not a dime's worth of difference between the two.' I read often in *World* concern over losing the Senate, House or White House to Democrats, but wonder if it really makes any difference who is in control?"

I agree with Berglar that many Republicans have been disappointing. Still, here's my short list of where we'd be domestically if liberal Democrats had controlled all branches of government over the past two decades: Over three million abortions per year. Euthanasia rampant. Gay "marriage" legal everywhere. Home schooling illegal. Christian schools facing severe restrictions. Propaganda in public schools more virulent. Tax rates higher. Nationalized (and poorer) health care our only choice.

The GOP, for all its weaknesses (and the tendency of some Republicans to back the liberal agenda), has helped to keep some of those developments from occurring. Does offering that list mean that *World* is a GOP front group? No way. *World* has criticized GOP leaders on many issues. We are journalists, not courtiers, and we try to follow biblical principle rather than particular princes.

I've personally felt the challenge. I helped a little in developing the compassionate conservative vision, but when it was necessary to decide in 2000 whether to be a journalist or a TeamBush member, I chose journalism.

The Bush folks were nice, although I suspect relieved that someone who excited virulent liberal opposition did not ask for a job. Shortly after inauguration day Karl Rove took me to his office (formerly Hillary Clinton's) and showed me her hidden vanity mirror. Then I irritated the Administration by journalistically questioning aspects of its faith-based initiative, and haven't been back to the White House for a while. No problem: After receiving a lot of attention during 1995 and 1996, and again in 1999 and 2000, I've learned that I can take it or leave it.

Does the Democratic Party have some honest candidates and does the GOP have some slimeballs? Of course, and I will not vote for a candidate I know to be an unrepentant adulterer or a major league liar. But political correctness dominates Democrats more than it does Republicans, and PC pandering leads to dishonesty. Liberal teachers' unions are so influential in the Democratic Party that it can't see straight on educational choice. Al Gore's foreign policy would leave the US dependent on the UN Congressional Democrats are doing their best to eviscerate welfare reform and make more people dependent on the government once again.

As to George W. Bush: Even though I'd like him to push harder in several domestic areas, I'm so glad that he is president, and not only because of the usual policy concerns. Here's another personal story, about my one encounter with Bill Clinton. It came at the very end of 1997 at a "Renaissance Weekend," one of those affairs right before New Year's Eve that brought together over a thousand liberal friends of Bill and several conservatives such as myself. (We were entertainment.) When I had the opportunity to talk with Clinton one evening, I mentioned that I was writing a chapter on Henry Clay for a book on American leaders, and saw many Clay-Clinton similarities.

The president did not ask what the similarities were, or I would have told him: Henry Clay gave insinuating speeches in which he said, essentially, I feel your pain; other Americans saw him as smooth but untrustworthy; he was a bigtime womanizer. But Clinton did not ask. Instead he said, "That's such an interesting period of American history, I think about it all the time." OK. The next morning, while I was saying a few words about race relations and trans-racial adoption, Clinton wandered in and during the audience participation segment made a comment: "This is such a crucial matter for America. I think about it all the time." And so it went.

I don't know how many times Clinton told people he was thinking about their particular concern all the time—or how many times he did not tell people what he was really thinking about much of the time. What's the value of having an honest president like George W. Bush? It's priceless. And what's the value of having a Congress that's often disappointing but at least not dictatorially pushing a far left agenda? Certainly worth a minute in a voting booth. (2002)

Campaign Spending

Every reporter is trained to ask six questions: who, what, when, where, how, and why. The first five of those questions are asked regularly. The sixth is not. Ernest Hemingway once reminisced, "After I finished high school I went to Kansas City and worked on a paper. It was regular newspaper work: Who shot whom? Who broke into what? Where? When? How? But never Why, not really Why."

Conventional news organizations are now belatedly looking into Clinton administration fundraising scandals, but we are still getting only half-baked answers to the key "why" questions: Why did Clinton and Gore go where no men in their positions had gone before? And why does the political system make such tackiness the tactic of choice for those who place success above scruples?

On the first question, we're certainly seeing that Clinton and Gore are the leaders a lie-friendly society deserves. Already this year we've seen abortion industry spokesman Ron Fitzsimmons confess that he lied about the number of partial-birth abortions that occur each year. We've seen five women admit they were pressured by feminist-fearing Army investigators to cry rape untruthfully. In each case, those who came forward did so because lying bothered them—but what about all the folks who have Kevorkianed their consciences?

The second question is tougher: Why are campaigns financed this way? There is individual culpability, sure. Some new rules may be needed, sure. But there is a more basic problem when even US senators need tens of millions of dollars to run for jobs that pay $133,000.

Inquiring minds should be asking: Why all this spending anyway? Why do contributors drop a thousand here and a hundred thousand there?

Many do it because they are making an investment, and they expect the investment to pay off a goodly percentage of the time. In the nineteenth century Britain's Lord Acton offered his dictum: Power corrupts, absolute power corrupts absolutely. Power-embracing corruption is not new in American history: power attracted bribes even in colonial days. But what we are seeing now, with so much power centralized in Washington, is that enormous power attracts enormous bribes.

We had a smaller version of this problem in colonial America. Then, royal governors and judges had the power to seize or affect private property through regulation, excessive taxation, and use of eminent domain. Colonial landowners who worked hard to improve the value of their property could see it seized from them in the name of the public good. In that environment, astute citizens often felt they had no choice but to pay off magistrates or officials.

That all changed with the coming of the Constitution. Newly-independent Americans asked why bribery occurred, and then refused to ban political contributions. Instead, they limited government power (and bribe-taking potential) through a variety of means. They emphasized, in Article 1, Section 10 of the Constitution, that legislators could not pass laws "impairing the Obligation of Contracts." They refused to give federal officials power to grant charters of incorporation, build canals, regulate transportation, establish a national university, or create institutions that furthered literature and art.

Overall, the founding fathers took to heart James Madison's argument that liberty was best-protected not by restricting private interests, but by letting them compete freely and then counterbalance each other, so no one would become too powerful. Throughout the US's first century, court interpretations prohibited states from nullifying private agreements in the name of the "public interest," so there was less reason to bribe officials. Instead of restricting private ability to contribute to campaigns, the founders made it less significant to do so.

They did not eliminate bribery. Given the corruption of human nature, it would be unrealistic to expect that. But bribery on the federal level was contained, and vile administrations like those of U. S. Grant or

Warren Harding were the exception. Now, bribery and its kissing cousin, payment for "access," is the rule among Republicans and Democrats alike.

The way out is not today's conventional solution of imposing campaign spending limits, because that also means cutting into First Amendment guarantees of freedom of speech, including political speech. The better approach is to ask "why?" and then proceed to decentralization: Less power in Washington, less need to spend big bucks for bribes that by any name smell equally sour. (1997)

An Election Day Homily

In his just-published *Republican Theology*, Benjamin Lynerd takes aim at "the ideology of American evangelicals—a libertarian ethos combined with restrictive public moralism" on issues such as abortion. Putting aside momentarily whether support for unborn babies is "restrictive" or protective, what about Lynerd's basic point that limited government and biblical ethics are strange bedfellows?

He's wrong. That's because we can keep government small only when most persons honor their fathers and mothers while refraining from the practice of murder, adultery, theft, and false witness.

The reason for that is partly obvious. A high-crime society needs more police, more judges, more jails. Some effects are more subtle. If children don't honor their parents by caring for them when poverty and illness strike, Social Security and Medicare expand. When children are born out of wedlock or marriages breaks apart, or when affluent persons don't love their neighbors on the other side of the tracks, poverty (and demands for more governmental welfare) increase. When financial experts lie, economic losses and calls for more regulation grow.

Let's dive deeper. Southern Baptist Theological Seminary president Al Mohler, in one of his daily "The Briefing" podcasts, which I highly recommend, praised the Catholic Catechism's use of the term "intrinsically disordered" to describe some sexual practices. That's a good phrase, and it goes beyond sex: Intrinsic disorder seems to me a synonym for original sin. Remembering either of those two-word sets is helpful when we're tempted by either anarchy or socialism, both of which James Madison shot down in Number fifty-one of *The Federalist Papers*.

Here's what Madison (trained at college in Princeton by Presbyterian minister and Declaration of Independence signer John Witherspoon, now best known as an ancestor of actress Reese) wrote: "If men were angels, no government would be necessary. If angels were to govern men, neither external nor internal controls on government would be necessary. In framing a government which is to be administered by men over men, the great difficulty lies in this: you must first enable the government to control the governed; and in the next place oblige it to control itself."

Summary: Since men aren't angels, we need government. Since governors aren't angels, we need tight controls over government. We are, in two words, intrinsically disordered.

How much government do we need? Our Constitution's preamble states that the federal government is to "provide for the common defense." Given both radical Islam and the desire of oligarchs throughout the world to steal from others rather than build wealth through slow but steady work, we sometimes need to fight. The preamble then stipulates that the federal government should "promote the general welfare," and that's the great variable.

In America for three centuries strong families, churches, schools, and other civic organizations were the primary promoters of the general welfare. When those bulwarks splinter, government steps in, and power-seekers say they will bring order to our intrinsic disorder. Don't trust such promises. School superintendents distrust home-schooling and say we should rely on professional educators, as if they are immune from the Fall. Just about every television show and artistic production is pretty bad, due to our intrinsic disorder, so politicians give us a Public Broadcasting System or a National Endowment for the Arts, as if those producers are immune from the Fall.

We have crucial electoral choices to make just after Halloween, so aren't you tired of political commercials that proclaim one candidate will pass out candy to all, and the other is a ghoul? Let's get serious, and instead ask: Which candidates will acknowledge that we are disordered? Which see the importance of promoting the institutions that fight intrinsic disorder and eliminating or at least reducing the government-imposed obstacles they face? Which senators will fight the appointment of judges who promote disorder?

A secondary question: Which candidates are leading biblically-ordered lives? (If intrinsic disorder rules them they are likely to make new laws in their own image.) I've written books with bad titles, but I still like the title of one I wrote about eighteenth-century America: *Fighting for Liberty and Virtue*.

That fight goes on in 2014. Vote, please, not because politics is the antidote to intrinsic disorder, but because we need leaders who realize that government, while necessary, can't help us much—so they strive to protect groups that can. (2014)

Section Four:
Causes

Materialist philosophies that view human beings as machines or animals possess the high ground—academia, the most powerful media, many courts—in American society. For example, Americans have slipped into treating homeless people like pets, putting food in their bowls and giving them space in our kennels. But love without truth is a heresy, as is truth without love.

The heavens declare the glory of God, but the streets declare the sinfulness of man. Many societal problems start when we try to elevate our clan above other races, ethnic groups, cultures, or nations—but Christians, like Booker T. Washington more than a century ago and Hannah Hawkins more recently, fought that impulse in themselves and others.

Americans may think we're increasing compassion by making the concept synonymous with sympathy, but we're instead killing a good word by making it mean too much and thus nothing. We rarely challenge students to gain self-esteem by working hard rather than sitting back and garnering unearned praise. We train graduate students in graduate school intelligence, defined as the ability to make clever allusions in seminars.

It would be better to teach them how to ask tough questions and make discerning decisions: that's CEO intelligence.

Churches and Race

We regularly in *World* try to fight the myths that secular liberals promulgate concerning evangelicals.

For example, they say evangelicals want to legislate morality, even though we know that sin cannot be stopped by law because it is within everyone, and we know that real change comes one by one from the inside out, not million by million from the top down. We just don't want sin to gain governmental backing.

They say we're opposed to the First Amendment's guarantee of religious liberty, but we favor the free expression of religious beliefs in all areas of life, including business offices, governmental halls, and classrooms. They say we're gullible followers of potential dictators, but we are less likely than others to bow down to leaders because we obey a higher authority, and are taught not to put our trust in princes.

But one attack—that evangelicals are racially divided—does have a factual basis, as we can all see on Sunday mornings. Evangelicals understand that all people are created in God's image, yet we still almost always have white churches or black churches, not churches that reflect the diversity of heaven.

It's common for white evangelicals to say that discrimination against minorities is a thing of the past, something to cover during Black History Month (concluding next Monday) or Hispanic Heritage Month (in the fall) but not to think of as a Current Event. After all, the African-American and Hispanic middle class has expanded enormously, we've had two black Secretaries of State in a row, and minorities receive preferential treatment in many governmental programs.

That's not the way it looks from the other side, though. Southern Baptist Convention leader Richard Land mentioned to me earlier this month that most whites don't understand the daily exposure to racism, sometimes overt, usually subtle, that many African-Americans endure. He also spoke of the vast reservoir of good will toward blacks that exists among most American white evangelicals. He's right on both counts, and that means our goal should be to increase understanding so that the vast reservoir of good will is not a vast reservoir of cluelessness.

We should all start by asking and listening. We should ask about the comfort levels folks feel with members of different races: when there's discomfort, business deals are less likely. We should ask about the connections people use in gaining jobs or other opportunities.

I've been listening recently to my youngest son, age fourteen, who is black. (My wife and I adopted him when he was three weeks old.) We're living this year in an apartment complex in New Jersey where most of the kids his age are African-American, and they play a lot of basketball and sometimes walk together on streets. My son, who seemed not particularly race-conscious before, has good reason to believe that the local police treat him differently than they do white kids.

That experience has helped me to think about things I as a white person take for granted. I can go around in old clothes without having people attribute my lack of sartorial elegance to my race. I can arrive late somewhere without people believing that I'm lazy or have bad morals because of my race.

I still favor alternatives to governmental race-based preferences. For example, I believe that every economically-needy high school student in the top ten percent of his class or with SATs in the top ten percent of all test-takers should get a voucher equivalent to state university tuition, with that voucher usable at any public, private, or religious college. That would help poor blacks and Hispanics without redlining poor whites.

Since governmental quotas expand bureaucratic power, provoke a backlash, and are unfair to individuals, we need to find a better way to increase minority opportunities. The best way will be for Christians not to claim colorblindness but to admit our lack of it and strive to compensate. When exploring cross-race business and hiring opportunities, for example, we should ask ourselves not, "Do I feel comfortable with this person?" but "Why don't I feel comfortable with this person?"

As John Perkins and others have taught, we need to avoid both racism and bitterness about racism. The good news, as one of our blog contributors put it, is that in Christ "we all are red-skinned, covered by the blood that cleanses and forgives." (2005)

Racial Reconciliation

Racial reconciliation, as Promise Keepers and others have noted, should be high on the agenda for American Christians. But the drive for reconciliation, like many other things, can be based on God's wisdom or modern man's.

That drive for reconciliation can emphasize the importance for all people of faithfulness in marriage, work, and worship. It can help us to identify each other not by the color of our skin but by the content of our belief. Or, it can lure those with guilt feelings to speak a form of cultural Ebonics by supporting programs of reverse racism and governmental aggrandizement.

Which way will we go? We learn what to do primarily from reading the Bible, but a study of history provides supportive detail. Today, February 1, is the first day of Black History Month, and it's important for Christians to turn this month not into a celebration of racial differences but a remembrance of the centrality of biblical values to Black progress from the 1860s through the 1960s.

One person's life and beliefs show that centrality particularly well: Booker T. Washington (1856–1915). Sadly, the man who was a role model for two generations of American blacks is often ignored these days, since his Christian values are not considered politically correct within most university departments of African-American Studies. (The perspectives from such programs trickle down to elementary schools.)

Christians cannot afford to ignore Booker T. Washington, because his teaching holds the key to true reconciliation. Booker (no last name at first) was born into slavery in 1856 and freed when the war ended, only to find himself at age nine working in the salt mines of West Virginia. This side-effect of liberty taught young Booker that abstract rights did not preserve him from a shift in the mines that began at 4 a.m. He had to gain knowledge and work himself up from slavery, whether legal or economic.

Providentially, help came. Just as many inner city parents work extra shifts to pay tuition to a Christian school, so Booker's mother and other poor parents hired a literate black ex-soldier to teach their children how to read. Booker studied as soon as he got off work each day, and was ready in 1872 to walk most of the way to Hampton Institute, a new high school for blacks 500 miles away.

Booker arrived at the Institute in clothes he had worn for weeks and received an unusual admissions test: The head teacher told this unlikely-looking scholar to sweep and dust an adjoining classroom. He swept it three times, dusted every inch of wood in the room four times, and then—holding his breath—asked for an inspection. The teacher examined every corner and rubbed her handkerchief on the table and benches; finding it spotless, she turned to him and said, "I guess you will do to enter this institution."

Washington later remarked that those words made him "one of the happiest souls on earth. The sweeping of that room was my college examination, and never did any youth pass an examination for entrance into Harvard or Yale that gave him more genuine satisfaction." He then worked his way through Hampton by doing janitorial work, and eventually became a teacher there.

After nine years of work and study, the twenty-five-year-old Washington was ready to set out on his own in 1881, when he was invited to head a new school in Alabama, Tuskegee Institute. Visiting nearby families, he encountered one young black who had been to high school and was sitting in greasy clothes amid garbage in his shack, studying a French grammar rather than working the fields. Washington's initial program of study was different: He lined up the students and led them in a "chopping bee," during which he and they cleared the undergrowth, trees, and shrubs off land that was then to be used for planting food crops.

Some of the students protested, arguing that they had come for an education so they would not have to do manual labor, "slave work." Washington, however, swung his ax vigorously, both showing and telling that "There is as much dignity in tilling a field as in writing a poem." Dignity, he taught, came from glorifying God in whatever capacity He placed us, and then working to improve our circumstances. (1997)

African-American Success

Black History Month in Austin, Texas, began terrifically with a February 1 gospel concert at the University of Texas. The concert was a tribute to one man, Elmer Akins, who has set a record—fifty years—for consecutive hosting of a gospel music show on one Austin radio station. It also highlighted the singing of a group that first became known four decades ago, The Mighty Clouds of Joy.

Such records of perseverance are impressive, yet many of the performers on February 1 stressed not the glory of music but the glory of God: They were excited about being able to "lift up the name of Jesus" at a state university largely hostile to Christianity. For one night at UT, "diversity" meant consideration of not only race but religion, with Christ freely praised.

As I have written throughout this month on this page, Black History Month is worth celebrating, and Bible-based lessons taught by Booker T. Washington (1856–1915) are worth remembering. Often, however, those lessons are forgotten. Often, African-American Studies departments at major universities blame slavery for social problems that exist in black communities—conveniently forgetting that, through the teaching of Washington and others, those problems had been reduced tremendously by 1960.

For example, as Thomas Sowell has pointed out, each of the first five decennial censuses taken after Washington's death—those from 1920 to 1960—showed that at least sixty percent of all black males at least fifteen years old were married. Each ten years the percentage of blacks who were married increased, as did the rate among whites. The difference between black and white rates of marriage was always less than five percent throughout that period.

If blacks from 1960 on had continued making social progress at the same rate as they had over the earlier decades of the century, black poverty by now would be unusual, and the economic despair that now dominates many urban communities would be rare. Sadly, as blacks jumped over legal and political barricades during the 1960s, some thought they could ignore Booker T. Washington's wisdom.

By 1980, fewer than half of all black males age fifteen and up were married, and the gap between white and black marriage rates had risen to seventeen percent; by 1992 the gap was twenty-one percent. This is crucial because race makes far less difference in income than family composition: white, female-headed families are twice as likely as black, two-parent families to live in poverty.

Other statistics also show the importance of Booker T. Washington's emphasis on marriage, family development, and education. As Sowell notes, as early as 1969 black males who came from homes where there were newspapers, magazines, and library cards had the same incomes as whites from similar homes and with the same number of years of schooling. By the 1980s, black husband-and-wife families where both were college educated and working earned slightly more than similar white families.

Many blacks, of course, have taken Booker T Washington's advice, and they are doing well. But others who grew up in the God-is-dead 1960s (and their children) fell prey to a revolution in values. With less affluence to start with, blacks generally had less of a margin of error. Middle class white kids could do drugs as a lark and then return to sobriety, but many poor black kids who fell behind never caught up.

Since the sixties, of course, single-parenting has increased throughout our society, but most dramatically among blacks. Public schools have gotten worse: That's exactly what we would expect when discipline erodes and a lack of competition protects oldline monopolies. Many black children grow up under horrendous circumstances, their bitterness fanned by those who, as in Washington's time, politically and economically profit from tearing down rather than building up.

The positive lessons of Black History Month will take years to put into practice, but they are conceptually easy. Churches that teach the whole counsel of God concerning life both in this world and in the next are crucial. Access to better schooling, which for millions of children will require development of either private scholarship or public voucher programs, is essential. It is vital for good students to go to college and major there not in African-American Studies but in accounting or engineering or other fields of knowledge that help them to build businesses.

At the end of this century, as at the beginning, Booker T. Washington's recipe for progress can be encapsulated in twelve words: Build strong churches. Build strong families. Build strong schools. Build strong businesses. Amen. (1997)

Telling Kids Their Armpits Stink

I often edit better and occasionally think better by keeping a particular person in mind.

For years in editing *World*, one of our readers, a fifty-year-old dentist, appeared to me: Smart and busy, thoughtful but not academic, he wanted to think Christianly and valued a magazine that helped him to do so without wasting his time.

For years in evaluating poverty-fighting groups, I thought about heroic Hannah Hawkins, the widow of a husband murdered in 1969. For thirty years, from 1985 until the last few months, she ran Children of Mine, an after-school program for 50–100 kids in Anacostia, the part of Washington, DC, that tourist guides ignore.

During visits over the past two decades she taught me to look beneath the surface of glowing programs. On one visit she had just come back from a government-sponsored meeting about Southeast Washington revitalization. She fumed, "The beautiful people were there, looking for money. Just like the War on Poverty, money went into the pockets of the greedy. These folks are ready to clean up—unless stuff gets funky. Then they call me in to be the clean-up person."

The old building that housed Children of Mine was crowded. The roof sometimes leaked. A realistic soundtrack for her program would feature chattering kids but also police sirens and, occasionally, gunshots. But Hawkins scowled about opportunities to send kids to nice facilities. She'd get invitations for them to show up on days when officials were visiting and host programs wanted to create the illusion of vibrant activity. She called that "pimping" her kids. She declared, "I will have no part of that."

Why did children flock to her when she commanded them, "Wash those dirty hands"? Why, when she told a preteen, "Your armpits stink. Wash them before you come tomorrow"? But that boy meekly said, "Yes, ma'am." They obeyed because most of the adults they knew were selfish, but Miz Hawkins wanted what was best for them. "I ain't easy to deal with," she said, "but my children know I love them and care about them." Her goal was to bring them "from disgrace to grace."

She often gave children maxims such as, "Stay on the street called straight . . . Get that ugliness off your face . . . People who pick fights end up dead or in jail." She wouldn't accept government money because "couldn't have prayer." Besides, when she once agreed to take federally supplied meals, "The milk was warm, the tacos were cold, and the watermelon was sour."

Hawkins, a handful of volunteers, and some donors made it possible for her to lead Bible studies, tutor children, and give them grammar lessons along with a meal: "I need one person to tell me what a verb is." Money was tight but she hated waste and told of official anger when she didn't give milk to children who didn't want milk: "They said I didn't give the children complete meals. I said I wanted to teach the children not to waste." She scorned the government response: "Give it to them anyway. Give them a complete meal, and let them throw it in the trash."

Hawkins went from age 55 to age 75 during the time I knew her, but seemed ageless. She died of cancer on May 7. Sixteen days later *The Washington Post* reported her demise. That's better than my record of not hearing the sad news until June 17.

She was not a favorite of child advocates on the left, so she often went unnoticed by all except the children she saved. One scene of *The Right Stuff* (1983) shows reporters asking astronaut Gordo Cooper who was the greatest pilot he ever saw. Cooper starts musing about pilots at a base in California's high desert, far from the publicity spotlight . . . and some of them crashed and had their photos on the wall of a bar that burned down . . . and he starts to give the name of the greatest, Chuck Yeager—but the reporters are impatient.

Yeager, at least, is famous for breaking the sound barrier, and he did a commercial for batteries. Hawkins helped the children she mentored break through barriers, but she had no commercials and made no money. Still, she's the best anti-poverty warrior I ever saw. (2015)

Bait and Switch on Homelessness

Do hemlines go up or down with Republican presidents? When the Yankees win the World Series, is that good or bad for the stock market? A lot of the correlations made by folks looking for headlines are silly, but one seems to be holding true: A rising GOP tide lifts all press stories about homelessness. The same sad people ignored by reporters during the Clinton years are now sought out for their views on heartless conservatives.

Yes, it's time once again for the poverty-fighting Bait and Switch. Attract caring people to liberal causes by preaching that they can change the lives of the homeless for the better by passing a multi-million or billion dollar (who's counting?) piece of legislation. Watch while nothing changes or—more often—money allocated for those who fail tempts more people to give up fighting and plop into the safety net. Then switch the proselyte to a position even further to the left: lack of success means that the government must double its spending.

But reality has a way of biting. Half a millennium ago church leaders in Lyons, France, decided their parishioners did not have enough opportunity to save themselves years in purgatory by performing the good deeds of offering alms to the poor. So the Lyons bishop sent messages to his counterparts in other cities: Send us your beggars. And so it was: homeless men from all of Europe came, begged, drank, and died. They kept coming, until the bishop begged, no more.

San Francisco is a Lyons of the present, offering its thousands of single, homeless residents $320–390 per month, plus food, shelter, clothes, and medicine. That stipend, supplemented by panhandling, enables the homeless to stay in misery and—according to National Public Radio—helps to "preserve the city's reputation for compassion." So some propose to cut the monthly stipend (often used for drugs and alcohol) to $50: NPR says that is a "punitive approach."

But what's compassion? San Francisco compassion, according to the *Christian Science Monitor*, means that "urinating in public is a cherished right." San Francisco compassion means that 183 homeless people died on the streets in the year 2000, the victims of drugs, alcohol, and what President Bush accurately calls the soft bigotry of low expectations. The *Monitor* portrayed one San Franciscan "looking at a panhandler wrapped in a tattered and filthy blanket" and saying, "This guy here, you can't get him to follow somebody else's rules." So, rather than trying, give him $320–390 each month and watch him die.

NPR says the problem of homelessness is complicated, and it is, but part of it comes down to this question: Should homeless individuals have to follow somebody else's rules? Just about all of us have to do exactly that. "It's not tough to be homeless in San Francisco," the *San Diego Union* quoted one of the Bay Area's homeless men as saying. It's tough for those with little willpower to leave homelessness, because city support plus panhandling allows them not to follow somebody else's rules.

Today's homelessness debate is not about caring. The liberal position is a classic bait and switch. The bait is "don't be mean-spirited," and those thus hooked are eventually switched to a perverse definition of liberty. When Patrick Henry said, "Give me liberty or give me death" he was not talking about the liberty to urinate in public or sit around without using any of his God-given talents. He was not talking about the social equivalent of ignoring the law of gravity. But San Francisco compassion today demands that anyone can choose any lifestyle he chooses, no matter how destructive, and have taxpayers pay for it.

We should say no to such a reality-denying manipulation of sentiment. Homeless individuals who want to change their lives and begin acting responsibly deserve support. Those who are psychotic and unable to change their lives deserve help. Those who disable themselves need not a road to further destruction paved with a few dollars, but true compassion, which means seeing them as created in God's image and helping them to restore that shine, no matter how many layers of caked-over dirt are in the way. (2001)

Population

The date of this issue, April 22, throws me back to when I was in college thirty-six years ago and we observed the first Earth Day on April 22, 1970. The celebration gained wide backing that year for reasons as polluted as the rivers that needed cleaning. Some supported it out of fear of over-population. Richard Nixon publicized it in the hope that students who spent time on ecology would have less time for anti-war demonstrations.

Some Christians—I was not one at the time—became involved for the right motives. They understood that God made Adam a gardener, calling him to take the raw materials of nature and make them more beautiful and more productive. Early this month New York City pastor Tim Keller offered an excellent exegesis on this theme to a group in his city. He observed that many people, including venture capitalists, are gardeners, taking the bare materials of the world and adding value.

God wants us to be fruitful and multiply, but after hearing Keller point out that gardeners do not grow on trees, I thought more about God's methods. To help us produce gardeners, He provided incentives such as sex and the expectation of old age. Within marriage, if it feels good, do it—and behold, a certain percentage of unions will multiply the population. Within the aging process, folks who knew they eventually would weaken wanted children who could support them down the road.

Over-population fanatics a generation ago, forgetting that every "extra" mouth brings with it one more pair of hands, ardently tried to make big families unfashionable. They were aided by the removal of the age-old incentives. Effective contraception offered sex without reproduction (and abortion became a backup). Social Security offered retirement income without reliance on children. Sure, other incentives remained: Kids are fun, it's satisfying to watch them mature, and God says all that is good. But with sex and security no longer tied to procreation, many couples had one child instead of four.

Over the years the separation of sex and security from reproduction has trimmed but not stopped US population growth, because the United States is the most religious country in the West, and many people still have the faith to have children. We've also learned that affluence and ecology are not at odds: A rich country can afford environmental protection.

Many de-Christianized European countries have shrinking populations. The 20 million or more immigrants who do Europe's dirty work are from Muslim countries and therefore much harder to absorb. The Ottoman armies centuries ago could not get past the gates of Vienna, but the demographic changes make Europe ripe for Islamic takeover during this century.

Similar population concerns have now led to an immense policy change in Israel. Demographers predicted that Israel, if it annexed the West Bank, would eventually have an Arab majority. Most Israelis shuddered, said they could not allow that to happen, and voted to hand over territory to Palestinian terrorists. Japan, although not threatened by invasion, is having its own anguished debate as a census unveiled earlier this month showed a decreasing population.

I'm not, let me emphasize, arguing against contraception used by married couples who have been fruitful or plan to multiply. (Other Christians differ on that, and we should respect each other's positions.) Nor am I saying it's necessarily wrong to have government stipends for the elderly. (Some Christians disagree.) My point is that massive social changes have consequences unanticipated by planners but predictable by those who, because of biblical teaching, discern the nature of man. Children are a blessing but also a lot of work, and our sinful nature is to be risk-averse unless material benefits are evident.

This puts a different spin on Christian calls for societal revival. We normally speak of the need to be born again to attain eternal life in heaven, and that is true. But cultures that have been Christian and are now losing population need to be born again through a new Reformation that would once again emphasize God's command to be fruitful and multiply gardeners. A nation that is not born again will eventually die, and its environment will revert from garden to wilderness. (2006)

Environmentalism

America is land of enormous natural beauty. I first began to comprehend the size and loveliness of the United States in the summer of 1971 while bicycling across the country, Massachusetts to Oregon, rolling through fruited plains and feeling in my legs and lungs the majesty of purple mountains.

I recommend slow travel of that kind, but such a trip is not in everyone's comfort zone. (It's not even in mine any more, as I hit fifty this month.) Minivans and SUVs are the way to go for millions of Americans. Growing affluence enables many families to go further and see more than would otherwise be practical for them—but some essentially say that we should travel slowly and uncomfortably, or not at all.

General affluence, we are told, leads Americans to pollute more, endanger more wildlife, and use much more than our share of the world's resources. The books of Paul Ehrlich and other ecological fatalists are still on high school and college reading lists. Even though predictions of worldwide famine and resource scarcity have been as inaccurate as the dire Y2K prophecies, mistaken environmentalist doomsayers are still on media call lists.

But slowly, a new understanding is developing. I'd summarize it this way: It isn't economically easy to be green. The natural tendency of people is to pollute. For example, primitive biomass fuels like wood and dung are the typical first choices for cooking and heating, and they pollute the air, Cutting down trees, apart from careful planning and replanting, depletes resources. Affluent cultures move past reliance on wood, but that takes time and money.

The new paradigm acknowledges that we are environmentally wasteful in many ways, but argues that affluence gives us the opportunity to be less so. Affluence allows us to produce more of the goods and services that help to improve the human condition, and also to alleviate the negative effects of much past pollution. Technological innovation and the growth of human capital lead to improvements in both the environment and the economy.

I don't know enough to judge firmly whether the "affluence is environmentally good" theory makes more sense than the "affluence is environmentally bad" conventional wisdom. But, if it does, the conventional green tendency to oppose economic progress in the name of environmental stewardship is sadly self-defeating.

I do know, given man's sinfulness, that better things often do not make for better living. Advancements in agriculture, industry, and commerce help to minimize pollution and transform waste products into efficiently used resources, if people have spiritual and economic incentives to be stewards. The Soviet economic and environmental disaster shows what can happen when biblical and free market incentives are missing.

And I know absolutely what the Bible teaches: that human beings are created in God's image and are thus the most valuable resource on earth. Blessed is a country whose quiver is full. Full of people. Full of flora and fauna. Full of life. People made in God's image have some creative power. As gardeners we can add to the earth's abundance, not merely live off the land.

The Bible teaches that human beings have an obligation to be stewards and gardeners in a way that benefits other men and women and also other creatures. We're not supposed to leave oxen and donkeys in the ditch, even if those animals are owned by enemies. We're not supposed to cut down fruit trees even in times of war, when cutting down an enemy's trees might be to our military advantage

The Bible teaches that the affluent, while not necessarily their brothers' keepers, should certainly be their brothers' helpers. Those who own fields are to allow the hungry to glean in them. Those with political power should not use it to impede the poor by denying them the opportunity to move out of poverty.

Do we move perilously close to denying opportunity when we try to impose the environmental standards of the affluent on people in other nations who are desperately trying to break out of poverty? Do we despise the poor when we put more emphasis (as was the case in Austin several years ago) on an endangered species of cave spiders than on safety for people in the poorer part of the city who are endangered by crime-ridden streets? If we embrace environmental romanticism, believing that "nature knows best," are we losing the opportunity to develop and use innovations that could help millions of the earth's inhabitants, human and animal?

Those are questions to ponder as we enjoy God's provision this summer. (2000)

Endangered Spiders,
Endangered People

As Congress takes another look at the Endangered Species Act and other matters of environmental legislation, I'd like to take a look at this national issue from the vantage point of my Austin, Texas, neighborhood.

In Austin, a southern fried university town/state capital seasoned by country music and computer plants, conventional environmentalists are always discovering various endangered species of spiders, toads, and fish, and then getting the city council to spend money on buying land or developing programs to save them. In the meantime, our urban core is disintegrating.

My neighbors and I care about our local environment, and we are fed up with environmentalism. This hit home last month when, not far from my home, a sixty-year-old deaf woman was murdered. Alma Jean Ward died on a Saturday evening when she walked out of a convenience store, unaware that rival gang members were shouting at each other in the parking lot. When the shouting turned into shooting, she died in the crossfire. The corner where she died has been an illegal drug market for years, but a police presence has been rare—higher government priorities elsewhere, we were told.

My family and I have lived in our majority-black, mixed middle class-and-poor neighborhood since 1984. Until recently our environment was generally safe. I remember, a few years ago, going "down the creek" with my kids, which meant hiking along a tiny creek that adjoins our backyard and empties into a larger one, and then looking for fossils in an area where that creek widens out. It was like being in the country, but a dozen minutes from downtown.

The water was not pure, but this environment was still pleasant. Same thing about the streets my wife and I have walked along a thousand times, exchanging hellos with other walkers and letting our dogs sniff each other. Our neighborhood was and is not Eden, but homeowners of diverse incomes enjoyed large, tree-filled backyards, with well-constructed houses terrific for large families—terrific, that is, as long as the surrounding environment was free of terror.

My wife and I remember neighborhood association meetings as models of citizen participation. It sounds corny, but think of a Frank Capra movie or a Norman Rockwell painting, yet with faces of varied hues, and you can imagine the pleasure of whites and blacks expressing not racial bitterness toward each other but a common desire to maintain a safe environment. And often, there was a common request to city officials: Help us to preserve our diverse environment. Make civic safety your top priority.

Are the good times in our neighborhood over? We and others are asking that question, because last month's murder shows how close our environment is to becoming crime-ridden. My neighbors say things like, "How many tragedies are we going to have to endure before someone gets serious? . . . We need more police protection. We get ignored . . . The environmentalist side of town doesn't care about our environment." Folks feel that if Austin's politically-potent "tree huggers" had paid attention to the need to protect endangered humans, Alma Jean Ward would probably be alive today.

Liberal environmentalists, of course, says it's not an either-or situation: Agree to raise taxes, and you can protect people along with flora and fauna. But taxes already are high, and economic reality requires prioritization, not a back-scratching proliferation of programs. Liberal environmentalists also say that if we don't pay now we'll pay later, as we lose out on biodiversity. But it's hard to take that long view when drug dealers and gangbangers are threatening to wipe out the diversity of a neighborhood like ours and substitute a monoculture of despair.

Some Christian environmentalists see the limitations of liberalism, but others go with the crowd. Since conventional environmentalism involves calls for government action, education on the proper function of government also is needed. One Austin City Council member acknowledged, after the murder, a problem in spending $152 million "for birds and bugs" while cutting back on "cops on the beat." That council member admitted, "It's my fault, it's our fault . . . You let us screw you . . . Public safety is supposed to be our #1 priority. Let's deal with it. You make us cut somewhere else."

That's exactly right: Public safety is job one for the governing authority given the power of the sword, "for he does not bear the sword in vain. For he is the servant of God, an avenger who carries out God's wrath on the wrongdoer" (Romans 13:4). The most essential environmental spending is spending to protect life and liberty, including the liberty of individuals to enjoy their environment without risking their lives. (1997)

Immigration

As los presidentes Bush and Vicente Fox of Mexico meet this week, a three-dimensional national debate about immigration is intensifying, and a fourth dimension may soon kick in.

The three now-prominent dimensions are economic, political, and environmental. Economically, immigrant labor is important in many industries, but it apparently reduces wages for the native-born by several percentage points. Politically, TeamBush wants to increase its percentage of the Hispanic vote, but since most Hispanics are not Republican the conservative newsweekly *Human Events* had a front page headline, "Legalizing Illegals May Lead to Democratic Domination."

The environmental dimension is also significant, leading many Americans to temper sympathy for people searching for a better life with calculations about resources and a reduction of wide-open spaces. But a fourth dimension up to now hasn't received much notice. At *World* we always ask whether the Bible suggests ways to think through policy issues.

It turns out that biblical pleas for the kind treatment of aliens are almost as abundant as calls for the protection of widows and orphans. Prophets frequently commanded not to oppress the widow or the fatherless, the alien or the poor (Zechariah 7:10). Aliens in ancient Israel had the same opportunity as the local poor to take on some hard tasks, such as picking up grain from the corners of fields and picking fruit from high branches. Charity is also important: Israelites were to give part of their tithes to "the [alien], the fatherless and the widow, so that they may eat within your towns and be filled" (Deuteronomy 26:12).

The Bible emphasizes hospitality, but it also celebrates a melting pot. After all, the Bible's most famous story about an alien stars Ruth, the widow of an Israelite who had moved to the land of Moab and married her there. Three times Ruth's mother-in-law, Naomi, tells Ruth not to become an immigrant to Israel. Only when Naomi realizes that Ruth is determined to go with her, and only when Ruth says "Your people will be my people, and your God my God," does she assent.

Immigration to America used to be the secular equivalent of that. Aliens, like my grandparents, worked to learn English and wanted their children to be Americanized. Now, though, Mexican flags lead Los Angeles parades and naturalized US citizens from Mexico are encouraged to vote in Mexican elections. School multicultural programs teach kids to think of themselves primarily as members of a particular ethnic group rather than as Americans.

Two particular policy measures seem to be consistent with a biblical way of thinking. Israelites were repeatedly told, "You shall not oppress a hired worker who is poor and needy, whether he is one of your brothers or one of the [aliens] who are in your land within your towns." Illegal aliens today are easy to take advantage of, because they cannot contact their local sheriff when they are cheated. That's an argument for a a guest worker program, with temporary visas, so that those determined to come anyway gain legal protection and the right to work at jobs that would otherwise go unfilled.

Secondly, Ruth in the Bible book by that name receives help from a distant relative, Boaz, her "kinsman-redeemer." Immigrants to America have also had to have a sponsor who would teach them the ways of the new country and guarantee that they will not need to go on welfare. From the 1960s through the mid-1990s sponsorship agreements were often wishes rather than legally-binding obligations. Now they are being taken seriously again, and that is as it should be.

I could insert lots of caveats and cautions, of course. We need to stress biblical moral law and the principles of ancient Israel's civil law, but not the specific measures. Societies two-to-four millennia ago did not have the same kind of borders we have. In New Testament times, with Israel part of the Roman Empire, cultural barriers between Jew and Greek are addressed more than geographic boundaries, etc.

Even as we debate nuances, though, the Bible will help us remember that immigrants are important, sometimes in ways we don't anticipate at the time. The biblical Ruth was a successful immigrant and a romantic heroine who married Boaz, her deliverer. But she also became the great-grandmother of Israel's greatest king, David, and an ancestor of Christ Himself. (2001)

Immigration 2

It's almost Thanksgiving, when we remember how God blessed, and the Wampanoag people helped, a group of new immigrants to America. A month from now comes Christmas, when we celebrate the most sensational immigration of all time, the birth of Jesus.

Those events are worth considering as we examine the arguments about immigration today. Is it possible to take wise precautions against both terrorism and future disunity while honoring the pro-immigration flavor of American and biblical history? Let's look at the four types of anti-immigration arguments.

Type 1 criticizes not the immigrants themselves but a culture no longer committed to helping them assimilate. Some schools do a poor job of teaching immigrant children English, and thus limit their social and economic mobility. Some schools emphasize America's faults, instead of teaching that this country has accorded immigrants liberty and opportunity unprecedented in world history. Concerns about what we teach immigrants are valid if America is to become not a divided nation, but one still living out the phrase e pluribus unum.

Type 2 arguments emphasize homeland security. These also are generally valid. Given the backgrounds of the September 11 perpetrators, extra caution is in order when reviewing visa applications from countries that grow terrorists and do not crack down on them. The federal government must make our borders more than paper lines if it is to fulfill its constitutional function of providing for the common defense.

Type 3 arguments that favor restricting immigration to limit population growth are not as strong. Sure, we are to be stewards of God's creation and not overcrowd it, but this country still has a wealth of abundantly wide-open spaces. Urban areas are congested, but many small towns and rural areas are facing de-population. Ironically, the doors for immigration and abortion opened in the 1960s at around the same time, and in some ways the number of immigrants has merely replaced many of the babies who were killed before birth.

Type 4 anti-immigration arguments are really anti-immigrant arguments. We don't want those people, some say or suggest: They're not our kind. Among the murmurs: They're not used to democratic government, so they'll be easy prey for potential dictators. They're used to big government, so they'll vote for Democrats. They'll undermine America's Christian traditions.

This argument goes against American historical experience, which shows that those who have been denied liberties usually appreciate them the most. Yes, Democrats have gained most of the Hispanic vote in elections past, but they have also asked for those votes far more fervently. A survey by Latino Opinions shows two-thirds of Hispanics identifying themselves as pro-life. Now that President Bush is making Hispanic outreach a prime GOP task, voting patterns are beginning to reflect Latino values.

More fundamentally, surveys show three-fourths of Latinos, compared to 60 percent of Americans overall, saying that religion (almost always Christianity) provides considerable guidance in their lives. Hispanics are bolstering both Catholic and Protestant churches, with over one-fifth having converted to evangelical Protestantism. The recent influx of Asian immigrants has also helped churches. Korean-Americans are ten times more likely to be Christian than Buddhist, and other immigrants from Asia also often have Christian backgrounds.

But Christians have a reason deeper than such pragmatic considerations to welcome immigrants. Jesus, Mary, and Joseph were temporary immigrants in Egypt. Their ancestor, Ruth the Moabitess, had been welcomed to Israel over a millennium before. Christians, like Jews, are commanded to show hospitality to "the stranger within your gates." The New Testament emphasizes that "in Christ there is neither Jew nor Greek," and that we are to love our neighbors, regardless of national origin, like ourselves.

If Christianity is losing support in the United States, native-born Christians looking for culprits should look in the mirror. Two Zen Buddhist centers I visited recently were peopled by white Anglo-Saxon former Protestants. The Catholic priests involved in sex scandals uncovered in the last few years rarely have Hispanic names. Liberal denominations that are losing members—Episcopalians, United Methodists, and others—have been rocked by dissension over ordaining gays, not accepting immigrants.

Most of us can agree that immigrants should learn English but not the ins and outs of the welfare system. Let's institute anti-terrorist precautions while continuing to keep our doors at least half-open. Those who complain that more immigration will move America from its Christian past should realize that it might lead to a Christian future. (2002)

Immigration 3

LOWER EAST SIDE, NEW YORK CITY –This area dominated largely by immigrants for two centuries is a good place to think about America's growing immigration debate. This month dominated by two welcoming but challenging presidents, Washington and Lincoln, is a good time to do so.

The lower east side once was home to African-Americans freed from slavery, and then Irish, German, Italian, and Eastern European immigrants escaping from other forms of oppression. Now it has remnants of all those groups plus Puerto Ricans, Mexicans, Dominicans, Chinese, and other Asians.

A century ago a higher percentage of Americans had been born abroad than is now the case. Then, as now, immigrants suffered at first so their children could have better lives. Then, as now, work was hard and long for those who wanted to save some money. Then, as now, homes were crowded, with immigrants sometimes making a one-family apartment suffice for three.

But two differences stand out. One is that, in the past, leading institutions strove mightily to Americanize students. Walk to 45 Rivington Street here and see the five-story, red brick school where Harry Golden (originally Hershel Goldhirsch) enrolled in 1908. He later wrote a best-seller, *Only in America*, in which he didn't complain or blame the United States for the hard life immigrants had. Instead, he wrote, "the only thing that overcomes hard luck is hard work."

Other graduates of the all-boys P.S. 20 were acclaimed actors Paul Muni (Muni Weisenfreund) and Edward G. Robinson (Emmanuel

Goldenberg). George Gershwin (Jacob Gershowitz) showed the success of the school's attempt to inculcate a love for America culture when he composed between 1923 and 1935 *Rhapsody in Blue, An American in Paris,* and *Porgy and Bess.*

Just down the street at 61-63 Rivington stands the three-story, red brick building that was a New York Public Library branch funded by Andrew Carnegie and built with an open-air reading room on the roof. The patriotic books it stocked opened many minds: if it was typical of other libraries of the era, biographies of Washington and Lincoln were the most frequently checked-out works, and immigrants reading about the presidents would see how they treated newcomers to America.

For example, President Washington took his oath of office a couple of miles from here in 1789 and then wrote to one synagogue, "May the children of the stock of Abraham who dwell in this land continue to merit and enjoy the good will of the other inhabitants, while everyone shall sit in safety under his own vine and fig tree and there shall be none to make him afraid." The way to merit good will was to work hard to gain your own vine and fig tree and not to covet those of neighbors.

Abraham Lincoln opposed the "Know-Nothings" who made up part of the nascent Republican Party and applauded the contributions immigrants made. His 1864 Thanksgiving Proclamation gave thanks to "Almighty God" who "has largely augmented our free population by emancipation and by immigration." But he also expected new arrivals to be a blessing to America; for example, he praised German-Americans (then a leading immigrant group) because they were "true and patriotic."

That should be our test regarding immigrants. Those who come to America to tear it down or live off of others should not be welcomed. Those who are "true and patriotic" should be. This means we must toughen our tests for citizenship and not allow dual citizenship. It particularly means that our schools and libraries should do their part to communicate patriotism rather than politically correct anti-Americanism, and that all children should learn to speak English so we do not end up with a bifurcated culture.

I mentioned that there are two differences from the semi-good old days and here's the second: Then almost all immigrants came by boat through fixed entry points, and now we have porous borders with immigrants coming by land illegally. Now we are also stuck with a coalition of liberals who think immigrants can be their political salvation and corporate conservatives who see their economic usefulness.

I don't know the right number of immigrants to let in. I do know that those who are allowed in should be here legally, so that they have protection against those who would prey on them rather than pray with them. And I know that we cannot dodge this issue. (2005)

SECTION FIVE: CONCLUSIONS

Most religions are bad news, because they purport to teach people how to ascend to God—but if we're honest about ourselves and about the magnificence of the universe, we know we cannot climb high enough to meet a God who must be even more magnificent than His creation. The good news in the New Testament shows how God compassionately descended to us.

When Christians think biblically, we don't recruit followers by screaming that the sky is falling: we know that God holds up the sky. Some people jump off planes and others pack parachutes: both callings are essential. We can aspire to glorify God and enjoy Him forever without making Christianity merely a pie-in-the-sky faith, for "forever" starts right now.

Christians should recognize that America is not Israel: We live in a liberty theme park, not a holy land, and should enjoy an American diversity that goes far beyond race and ethnicity. We should embrace choice as long as all, including unborn children threatened with death, now or in the future get a chance to choose.

The World's Most Important Leaders

The letter from Sandra Garrison of Fayetteville, North Carolina was simple enough: "I enjoy your magazine, and appreciate the Christian viewpoint. I am an elementary school teacher. I'm writing to request a list of names of the most important world leaders and photographs of each if possible. Many thanks, in advance, from the young scholars who will benefit from your efforts."

At first I thought this one would be easy to answer. Most important world leaders, hmmm: List the alpha dogs from the US, China, Russia, Japan, Germany, maybe Britain and France and India. But then I started thinking about leadership and wondering: Why automatically race to government? What about business, organized religion, and other spheres?

Start thinking that way, and the list of possibilities grows. Bill Gates and other technological innovators/marketers. Billy Graham and John Paul II. Michael Jordan and Tiger Woods. Australian Rupert Murdoch, because of his media ownership in Europe and America. They've all led millions to look into their machines, their faiths, their styles, or their ways of presenting reality.

What about those whose ideas lead the leaders? Augustine, Muhammad, Adam Smith, Charles Darwin, and many others have led the way to changed understandings of how the world works. What of those who teach the leaders? And what about the adage, "the hand that rocks the cradle rules the world?" Aren't mothers the most important world leaders?

I started out purposely staying away from those with reputations only in one country, because the question was about world leaders. But, given the way American movies are watched around the world, what about Steven Spielberg? Given that people in many countries aspire to the life they see on America's leading television export, *Baywatch*, what about the producers of that show?

That train of thought, after making many stops, finally led me to the answer I'd like to offer to Sandra Garrison and her Fayetteville students. Because I've written about compassionate conservatism and my home in Austin is a convenient stop for foreign reporters assigned to make sense of our presidential election, I've been interviewed in recent months by journalists from twenty-three countries.

These reporters tell me that their countrymen know about Texas from having watched the television show *Dallas*. They know about Christianity in America from having seen some televangelist. Obviously, their readers are often mixed up, and the journalists themselves tend to look at America with jaundice and with awe. But here's what's vital: Almost all of these reporters say the United States is the most important country in the world today.

I don't think they say this just to flatter an American. I hope I do not believe them because of nationalistic arrogance. But I also believe the US is the most important country today, because we are the site of a vast experiment that the whole world is watching.

The most important country of ancient times was Israel. The laws laid down by Moses set up Israel to be a holy people separated from others and dedicated to God. The land itself was a theme park, with everything—geography, economics, laws, customs—stressing holiness. In the end, of course, the insufficiency of all those helps showed man's desperate need for Christ.

The United States is the most important country of modern times because America is a theme park devoted to liberty. We are the envy of much of the world because of the freedom we have to speak, write, worship, and work. We are free to build businesses and to travel. We are also free to consume pornography, practice adultery and homosexuality, and take advantage of others and ourselves. Other countries have their appeals, but for good reasons or bad, America has grabbed the imagination of the world.

Right now the future of our American theme park is very much in doubt. That's because a lesson regularly taught in the eighteenth century has now largely been forgotten: liberty without virtue becomes license, licentiousness leads to anarchy, and a reign of anarchy leaves the theme park in disrepair.

Who are the most important world leaders today? Those who will determine whether this nation, conceived in liberty but with a respect for virtue, will long endure. Those who will be free to do what they want but will know what not to do. Will they by grace do what is right, or will they succumb? That question is vital, for whatever path they take in our city on a hill will be watched around the world, and imitated.

Who are the most important world leaders today? Children of Sandra Garrison's class, look in the mirror. (2000)

Discerning Talent

Now that the school year has begun, seniors in high school and college need to think through what they will do once it ends. It's time, therefore, to present my four-step formula for thinking through careers: End, Talent plus Enjoyment, Talent, Employment.

I can explain the first part of the formula by quoting and applying the most famous question from the catechism of the Westminster Confession is, "What is man's chief end?" The answer: "Man's chief end is to glorify God and enjoy Him forever." In our careers, we glorify God by using full throttle, in godly ways, the talents He has given us. Since God does not give talent arbitrarily or willy-nilly—what He gives we should use—it's vital to find out what our talents are, because the existence of talent is a powerful way of ascertaining God's will for our occupational lives.

Discerning talent is easier said than done. Schools for the most part applaud generalists who can do well in a variety of subjects, but most occupations demand specialization: the ability to do one thing well. Grades used to be a powerful aid to discernment, but grade inflation now pushes teachers to deliver false signals. Out of ignorance or pseudo-friendship, few people are honest enough to call a splatter a splatter: instead, we tell those we like that they have created masterful paintings. It's important to find a mentor, colleague, or true friend who will be achingly honest.

Concerning enjoyment: since forever begins right now, we should derive satisfaction as well as sweat from the way we earn our daily bread (realizing that thorns and thistles will frustrate us at times). That does not mean we will be laughing all the way as we earn money to take to the bank. It does mean that if we're miserable on a job, sometimes we need to change our attitudes and sometimes our jobs (keeping in mind that, whenever possible, we should not leave one job until we have another).

Here's my possible leap of fatheadness: Most of the time the two questions—"What work am I good at? What work do I like doing?"—can be reduced to one, "What work am I good at?" That's because most of the time, if we're good at a particular occupation, sooner or later we will derive pleasure from our competence and from the feedback we get concerning our performance. To put it simply, we either like doing what we do well, or we grow into liking it. Of course, if young people don't enjoy a task, they will probably be reluctant to put in the time needed to further develop their talent—but my advice most of the time, when a person is talented in a particular field, is to stick with it.

I throw in lots of caveats, of course. By enjoyment, rightly understood, I don't mean a laff-a-minute, but long-term satisfaction. I distinguish between lawful and unlawful activities, and also tell young men that unless they are called to singleness, they will want an occupation sufficiently remunerative so their wives are not required to work outside the home when they have young children. I also offer a tie-breaker question to those rare individuals who have several areas of talent that they truly enjoy and are skilled in: Is there a particularly great need in one of those areas, perhaps because relatively few people have the talent and inclination to achieve great things within it?

But here's the summary: TE, talent and enjoyment, often comes down to talent alone, and then finding particular employment that fits a person to a T. God does not distribute talent by chance: if God gives someone a lot of something, it's not accidental, but a signal from on high that it should be used for God's glory.

Many students ask, essentially, "What do I want to be?" My suggestion is that God has in most cases already answered that question by handing out sets of talents and capacities. The better question to ask is, "What has God shown, by His distribution of abilities, that He wants me to be?" Some people react by saying, "But I may not like what God has chosen out for me." When a person is maximizing talents, he usually learns to like his God-arranged career, even if it might not be what he would have chosen for himself. A career does not need to be love at first sight. It does need to be a good match. (2002)

Parachute Packing

My dad was a metalworker when World War II began, working alongside his father making boilers for submarines. Because he was in a crucial industry, he was excused from the draft and could have sat out the war in Boston.

Instead, he enlisted to fight Hitler, and spent the last years of the war in England and then on the European continent, packing parachutes. Despite his admirable voluntarism, I remember as a child wishing, as children do, that he had been on the front lines like soldiers in the television show *Combat*, or like flyers in *Twelve O'Clock High*.

"When I was a child, I spoke like a child, I thought like a child, I reasoned like a child. When I became a man, I gave up childish ways" (1 Corinthians 13:11). When I became a man and learned more about how God places and uses various people, I started appreciating parachute packers.

Most jobs in our society are parachute-packing jobs, and few packers—whether they're executives or interns—become famous. Most of us know the names of some movie stars, but can we name a producer? We probably used soap this morning (come to think of it, maybe I didn't), but how many of us know the names of workers at Procter & Gamble?

Parachute packers who are Christians have a variety of attitudes toward Monday-through-Friday work. Some are at what I'd call level one, worshipping God on Sunday and packing the rest of the week to pay the mortgage. Others are at level two, seeing work as a way to pay the bills but also to earn money that they contribute to support pastors and missionaries, paratroopers seen as the real Christian fighters.

Those donations are good, but there's more to work than that. Level three parachute packers see the relevance of biblical commandments to job activities and try to constrain the sinful tendencies we all have. That's also good, but not enough. Sure, a person who doesn't steal (which includes making shoddy stuff), doesn't lie, and doesn't think murderous thoughts about some coworkers and adulterous thoughts about others, is way above average—yet what about coveting?

It's better to be on level four, where parachute packers see the workplace as God's gift of a venue for communicating the gospel to others and then—since talk is cheap—showing what difference a Christian understanding makes. For example, it's easy to practice *liberalitas*, which meant in ancient Rome helping those of equal or higher status so they in turn would proffer help. Biblical Christians over the centuries, though, have emphasized *caritas*, helping those lower in rank who could not return the favor.

Level four Christian parachute-packers earn money and show self-restraint, but they also give themselves away. Level four executives sacrifice themselves to make sure they'll be able to keep payroll checks flowing. Level four mail carriers, such as one I was recently blessed to have, joyfully drop off lots of envelopes and book packages—in my case, it helped that she's a *World* subscriber.

A level four view of the workplace begins with the realization that it, like everything in life, is an arena. That's because parachute-packers are not anonymous, even if no one recognizes their work. They work in front of spectators, the angelic hosts, and before one very special spectator, God Himself, who always provides opportunities to learn. (When things go right we can thank Him. When things go wrong we can recognize our own limitations and compare them to Christ's limitlessness.)

Much more could be said, but let me conclude with two personal notes. First, I appreciate our small band of *World* editorial folks, but without the people in *World*'s business office there would be no plane to jump out of and no parachutes carefully packed. So please remember to pray for and thank them.

Second, because I saw his detail-orientation in other ways later on, I'm sure my dad packed parachutes carefully, which means that some people in their 80s, and even more among their children born after the war, are alive today because of his conscientious work. Most of us do not do life-or-death parachute-packing, but it's good to remember that in our own lives something we do or say, perhaps even to a stranger, may become a parachute for someone in need—or a millstone around his neck. (2005)

Contentment

Ten years ago I ran across a program for adults with IQs far below normal that trained them to be baggers at supermarkets. What made the program work was its retraining component: Graduates of the program could do a decent job, but every few months they would start putting gallons of milk on top of bread, and would then need a refresher course.

That's the way many of us are when it comes to contentment. I'm generally very happy with the blessings God has given me, including a good wife, four fine sons, and a productive calling. Yet, every few months I do have a day of general discontent, and that's when I pick up a book that is a refresher course: Jeremiah Burroughs's *The Rare Jewel of Christian Contentment*, written in the 1640s but republished by Banner of Truth.

As Thanksgiving approaches, I recommend Burroughs because he has cogent replies to our typical reasons for not being thankful. Burroughs shows that we receive less punishment than our sins deserve, and that to be discontented in the midst of God's mercies, because we don't have even more, is wrong. He also offers each whiner a challenge: if you put all the afflictions in the world in one huge heap and divided them up equally among everyone on the globe, would you have fewer?

Burroughs writes about developing contentment during struggles by remembering how often God brings good out of hardship, and thinking of previous afflictions that proved beneficial. (This is good for a columnist who is struggling to get started; often the best columns are those that do not flow easily.) What about when we are physically uncomfortable? Burroughs notes that we are soldiers of Christ, and soldiers do not assume they will receive hot meals and a cozy bed.

And what if nothing good seems to be coming, and our reputation suffers? Burroughs notes, "If you hear others report this or that ill of you, and your hearts are dejected because you think you suffer in your name, your hearts were inordinately set on your name and reputation." Sometimes we need to have lower self-esteem: In the Old Testament, David reacted properly to Shemei, who scorned him, because he discerned that the mocker actually was God's instrument.

We fight discontent, in short, by keeping our chief purpose—God's glory, not our own—in mind. But that is so hard when probably the worst thing that can happen to a parent—the death of a child—takes place. Burroughs does not minimize how terrible that is by saying that God will use the death for good, although how that could be true is often beyond our understanding. Instead, Burroughs instructs us to remember the good that we are able to grasp: when King David heard of Absalom's death, he should have said, "O Solomon, my son, my son."

That is still hard to swallow: Time does heal deep wounds, but months or years often are necessary. The key to everyday contentment, however, is to remember that our internal state, not our external environment, is the chief determinant of our content or misery. Do we think we are discontent because we don't have enough goods? We should realize that taking in air does not satisfy the stomach, and taking in things does not satisfy the soul.

Burroughs provides the solution to discontent: "not in bringing anything from outside to make my condition more comfortable, but in purging out something that is within." Instead of buying a more prestigious car, purge covetousness by taking delight in what God already has bestowed on us. Instead of checking out Internet pornography, purge lust by enjoying rightful pleasures.

Easier said than done, according to those addicted to wrong. But Burroughs concludes his book with "considerations to affect the heart in any afflicted condition." As opposed to name-it-and-claim-it theology, he stresses that we should not presume on God: "Do not promise yourself great things." Instead, even if we don't get what we asked for, we should "make a good interpretation of God's ways" and thank Him for "the abundance of mercies" already bestowed. Good advice for all of us, when we start putting the milk on top of the bread. (1999)

Strength, Courage, Love

"Be strong and courageous," Moses tells all of Israel and then his successor Joshua (Deuteronomy 31:6, 7, 23). "Be strong and courageous," God thrice tells Joshua, and the Israelites say the same (Joshua 1:6, 9, 18). Later, King David gives Solomon that same exhortation, as does King Hezekiah his commanders (1 Chronicles 22:13; 2 Chronicles 32:7)

One principle of biblical exegesis is that a repeated statement is an emphasized statement. What then do we do with a phrase used at least eight times? Clearly, this is important stuff. But what does it mean to be strong and courageous?

To some it means confronting opponents of Christ on the street. Some activists say that in-your-face protests demonstrate true commitment, and those who speak within sanctuaries are wimps. They claim biblical warrant for yelling at people, "You're going to hell," because if they don't say it the heathen will never hear it. (As if gay newspapers haven't for years printed such comments in order to equate Christianity with hatred.)

I value guts and *World* wants to be edgy, but Christians should operate within the biblical context of what strength means. Paul the apostle tells the Corinthians, "Be strong. Let all that you do be done in love" (1 Corinthians 16:13–14). He tells the Ephesians, "Be strong in the Lord, and in the strength of his might" (Ephesians 6:10).

The strong perseverance of those who have led the solemn March for Life in Washington for thirty-two years is wonderful to see, and that's why we're glad to be picturing it on our cover this week. But

Christians who race out in glee to scream at their foes need some personal and theological maturing.

The folks who most exemplify for me strength in the Lord and letting all be done with love are those who serve at the front lines of poverty-fighting and pro-life work throughout the world—for example, Jim and Terry Cooney, the Maryland parents (*World*, Jan. 22) who adopt numerous children no one else wants and do so in the realization that there's no turning back.

The Cooneys have made commitments for a lifetime while trusting in God's providence. That doesn't satisfy some Christians who say they're only being Christlike if they follow His tough-talking example when confronting evil. Such claims, along with many others, should drive us to Scripture.

Certainly, Jesus was harsh to the ostentatiously religious—"you Pharisees cleanse the outside of the cup and of the dish, but inside you are full of greed and wickedness." He knocked those who invented laws beyond those biblically demanded: "You load people with burdens hard to bear, and you yourselves do not touch the burdens with one of your fingers" (Luke 11:39, 46).

Christ warred on those who should have been good shepherds, but He was gentle with wandering sheep and particularly with those outside of Israel, like the Samaritan woman (John 4) and the Syrophoenician woman (Mark 7). If more of us walked in His steps so that the typical secular college student associated Christianity with kindness and not contempt for others, evangelism would be much more productive.

Paul knew Phariseeism so well that he particularly emphasized the need to show and not harangue. One of the most-quoted Bible passages is what he wrote to the Corinthians, who lived in a port city that was probably one of the most ungodly in all of the Roman Empire: "If I speak in the tongues of men and of angels, but have not love, I am a noisy gong or a clanging cymbal" (1 Corinthians 13:1).

Corinthian Christians could have gone 24/7 protesting the decadence around them, but Paul pleaded with them to show love, which he defined as "not arrogant or rude. It does not insist on its own way; it is not irritable or resentful. . . . When I was a child, I spoke like a child,

I thought like a child, I reasoned like a child. When I became a man, I gave up childish ways" (13:4–5, 11).

For Joshua in his calling, strength and courage had an obvious military meaning—march into hostile territory and don't look back—as well as a spiritual one. But we are looking to Christ, not invading Canaan, so we are not here primarily to destroy: God does that quite well, thank you, by letting today's evildoers dig pits and fall into them. Our task is to build. (2005)

Were Christ's Words
UnChristlike?

A Kentucky Baptist preacher/weekly newspaper editor once told me how he ran out with his camera when he heard on a police band radio that a drunkard arrest was coming. Unlike Paris paparazzi he never chased anyone, but he did put photos of staggering citizens on his front page.

The preacher/editor told of how a man came to his office one day, pleaded with him not to publish embarrassing photos of his brother, and gave an emotion-grabbing reason for his request: "If you run those shots of Bubba, it'll just kill Momma." The editor replied, "Tell Bubba he better not drive drunk."

Did the preacher/editor lack love? Some—especially those who put bullet holes through his office window—said so. But the editor believed that if embarrassment could force a life-saving change in behavior, it would not be loving to look the other way. The same principle applies with other sins that we perceive, both in ourselves and others. We are not being kind to ourselves when we fool ourselves into thinking that wrong is right, nor are we loving others when we are not truthful. As Paul points out in 1 Corinthians 13:6, "[Love] does not rejoice at wrongdoing, but rejoices with the truth."

The first question for journalists, for ministers, and for all of us is: Do we love the people of God enough to bring the truth to them? A secondary question: How do we bring the truth to people? In a kind way, yes, but Paul's phrase about "speaking the truth in love" (Ephesians 4:15) is often taken out of context.

After all, one verse before his famous phrase Paul criticizes "human cunning, by craftiness in deceitful schemes." Those words do not appear particularly loving to some ears today. In case we still have any tendency to think sugarcoating is next to godliness, Paul provides a summing up in Ephesians 4:25: "Having put away falsehood, let each one of you speak the truth with his neighbor, for we are members one of another."

Christ certainly spoke the truth in love, but many of his statements were not sweet. From the gospel of Matthew alone it is easy to compile what some would call the un-Christlike sayings of Christ. Jesus called His opponents "ravenous wolves," "vipers," "hypocrites," "blind fools," and so on. When Peter acted wrongly, Jesus said, "Get behind me, Satan!" Nor were Christ's action weak: He loved the moneychangers when He used a whip to drive them out of the temple. He cared enough to tell them the truth about their actions and their need to repent.

There is of course a big difference between God's inspired words and ours, which often convey anger. Insisting that love and truth go together does not give us a license to speak the truth spitefully. But the tendency among many Christians today is to lean in the opposite direction: Love rules, truth loiters behind. We forget that love and truth can be like sodium and chloride. Love without truth is Satanic, and truth without love can also be poisonous. Sodium and chloride together make salt.

All Christians are called to be salty. Some are called to be watchmen. God tells us in Ezekiel 33 that when the watchman "sees the sword coming upon the land and blows the trumpet and warns the people, then if anyone hears the sound of the trumpet does not take warning, and the sword comes and takes him away, his blood shall be upon his own head. . . . But if the watchman sees the sword coming and does not blow the trumpet, so that the people are not warned, and the sword comes and takes any one of them, that person is taken away in his iniquity, but his blood I will require at the watchman's hand" (vv. 3–4, 6).

Speaking the truth in love means blowing the trumpet in a way that will wake up the sleeping. Few people enjoy being rudely awakened. I doubt if any drunks enjoy public embarrassment, but the Kentucky preacher/editor/watchman was speaking the truth in love as he plastered across his front page pictures of the plastered.

His readers learned a valuable lesson: If you don't want to be embarrassed publicly, don't do embarrassing things privately. The Latin expression *coram deo*, signifying "everything to be done in the sight of God," should be enough to keep us flying straight. When that does not happen, we need to show Christlike love by speaking Christ's truth. (1997)

Spotlighting Christ at Commencements

"**C**ongrats, seniors, this will be a heck of a graduation." That's how a New York University press release breathlessly announced the commencement snaring of US Supreme Court Justice Sonia Sotomayor. Other schools swoon over presidents: Barack Obama will speak at Barnard College (Columbia University) and Bill Clinton at little Columbia College in South Carolina.

Many universities think TV names make a heck of a graduation, so Tom Brokaw, Katie Couric, and Brian Williams are orating at prestigious schools, and CNN host/Time editor-in-large Fareed Zakaria is playing a Harvard and Duke doubleheader. Happily, some Christian colleges are counter-cultural: Biola students will hear artist (and *World*'s 2005 Daniel of the Year) Makoto Fujimara. Covenant College students will hear pastor Tullian Tchividjian.

Other Christian schools also show understanding that the primary purpose of their commencements is to glorify God who knit together each graduate, not to worship human idols. But commencement season has gotten me thinking about what the goal for all Christian speakers should be: Instead of plotting how to become more famous and sell more books, we should always aim to put the spotlight on Christ.

Spotlighting Christ means more than a lack of selfishness, because it also means not making our chief end the winning of support on a favorite issue. For example, let's say you can show that same-sex marriage is not good for children and even for the partners themselves. That's fine, but if you just use social science data to make your point, and leave out God because you don't want to upset anyone in your audience, you are worshiping created things rather than the Creator.

Natural law reasoning by itself is also useful but not sufficient for Christians, because our primary goal is not to glorify reason but to glorify God who created reason. Educated by pulp fiction and TV shows, we tend to think that a mystery is something solvable through reason, but in Paul's epistles (see Ephesians 3:3–6) only revelation can solve a mystery. That's certainly true about the mystery of marriage: If we don't recognize Christ's preeminence in molding a husband and wife over decades, our prattling about joyful lifetime marriage sounds like a fairy tale.

Seven chapters toward the end of Exodus make up one of those purportedly boring sections of Scripture, but they show well how revelation is the parent, reason the child. In the first six God tells the Israelites how to make and order the tabernacle, which will be the center of their worship in the wilderness. In the seventh, Exodus 31, God rests and says a team of craftsmen will "devise artistic designs," cut stones, carve wood, and so on, "according to all I have commanded." They are to use their reason in accord with God's revelation.

Natural law trumps positive, man-made law, and sometimes a reasonable examiner of human nature and society can discern valid moral principles. But since so much is mystery, the Bible trumps everything else, and Christian speakers should recognize that by citing facts but also pointing to Christ, the maker of facts. The best way to do that is debatable, and in-your-face rants before secular audiences are wasted opportunities, but so are academic speeches that sideline Christian commitment.

I'm not saying that God decreeth one particular style. I am saying that our goal is to show Christ's preeminence in all things. Will that emphasis hurt a speaker's attempt to win support for his particular issue or organization? Maybe, but is our chief end to win a particular debate or to help people embrace Jesus? When Johns Hopkins neurosurgeon Ben Carson (*World*, April 21) spoke at the presidential prayer breakfast in 1997 and at Columbine High School following the terrible shootings in 1999, organizers each time told him, "Don't mention Jesus." Both times he disobeyed: "If we are true Christians, we have to be willing to stand up for what we believe."

I've had that experience and come to that conclusion in lesser forums. It's nothing new. In Acts, chapter 4, rulers told Peter and John to stop talking about Jesus, but they responded, "We cannot but speak of what we have seen and heard." Commencement speakers who are Christians and are reading this: Please speak of Christ. It will be one heck of a graduation ceremony. (2012)

Resting in God's Grace

The Thanksgiving we'll celebrate later this month is a day for reunion but also disunion whenever Christians and non-Christians within a family gather around a big table. Especially if they live far apart, parents (or children) of unbelievers may feel they have to seize the time to press home evangelistic points.

I'm not against asking loved ones where they think they'll be if a car runs a red light and sideswipes them on the way home. It's a crucial question, but we shouldn't feel obligated to push and push as if the salvation of another rests on our shoulders. We should love those around the table and pray fervently for the Holy Spirit to work miracles.

As I've interviewed over the past decade prominent Christians with grown children, I've often asked (privately) whether their children are following Christ. Repeatedly, the answers have been: one is, one is not; or two are, one is not; or two are, three are not—and so on. When I ask if they can cite anything in their family or church environment that would explain the difference, they cannot.

The history of international evangelism is similar, writ large. Why did Christianity spread in Korea and not in Japan? Why a Chinese fizzling in one century and a wildfire in another? Yes, we can note social and geopolitical factors, including the growth of Christian belief in opposition to state-imposed Marxism, but all that is speculation. The most famous nineteenth-century missionary in Africa, David Livingstone, was directly involved in the conversion of . . . one man. Go figure.

On the last evening of a three-week trip this summer through seven Balkan countries, a Romanian friend asked me to speak to a group of

Bucharest intellectuals about what I had observed. I tried to beg off, saying any observations I might offer would be superficial, but he said I could be helpful in suggesting reasons for optimism.

That made my assignment particularly difficult, because during the three weeks I repeatedly heard pessimistic appraisals. Atheism has spread as young people see church hierarchs in cahoots with oligarchs. Many bright young people emigrate or hope to emigrate. Looking at political, social, and economic trends, it seems hard to be optimistic. But even if things were going well, Balkans residents would still depend on God's mysterious grace.

The secular equivalent of that mystery is the basis of many romantic comedies. For example, the good movie *Hitch* has as its main character, Hitch, a clever matchmaker who helps wealthy young men find romance with the women of their dreams. The film's plot emphasizes a hard case: a "Mr. Wide" wants to woo a beautiful actress. Hitch gives the fat guy a morsel of general encouragement that helps him summon up enough courage to make an initial impression on the actress. Then, things take off.

Surprisingly, the fat guy and the beautiful actress find they have common tastes and common insecurities. The romance develops without Hitch's involvement, until the actress learns that the fat guy had hired him. Thinking she has been manipulated, she yells at Hitch: "What did you do?" He thinks for a moment and honestly responds, "Nothing. Absolutely nothing."

I'm aware that some ministries promote methodologies they almost guarantee will produce results, but I'm skeptical: No one can corral the Holy Spirit. I've spent hours with individuals without result, yet one person who credits me with helping him come to Christ started on the path after a brief discussion in which we didn't even talk about God. What had I done? "Nothing. Absolutely nothing." God did it all.

This is not an argument for quiescence just because hard work guarantees nothing in salvation. I am suggesting that we think we're in control but we never are. Should that make us pessimistic? Nope: God's in charge, and God's in the business of mysteriously changing lives. That gives us hope around the Thanksgiving table.

By the way, David's Livingstone's brother-in-law, John Smith Moffat, also became a missionary unable to count many conversions. But an orphanage/school/work training program I visited several years ago in Zambia, Village of Hope, has changed the lives of hundreds. It had its start when three elderly Christian sisters, the grandchildren of an evangelist converted through Moffat's ministry, provided the land on which Village of Hope sits.

Go figure. (2014)

Avoid Spam Recruitment

Over the past decade *World* writers have regularly and justifiably praised Francis Schaeffer, who died twenty years ago after decades of promoting Christian worldview thinking. Schaeffer was particularly powerful in pointing out the hopelessness of non-Christian thinking, and showing logically why men and women should turn to Christ. What happens, though, when many people don't—and yet, in a democratic society, we need to work alongside them to counteract the aggressiveness of secular liberal absolutism?

Schaeffer noted the importance of developing "co-belligerency" contacts in those situations—but didn't spell out how far to go. The problem is great, and not only because in a fallen world social entropy rules, with idealists becoming dictators and democracies turning into kleptocracies. A more basic problem is that what makes sense to those with faith in God will often seem like nonsense to others. When Paul in ancient Athens spoke of the resurrection that many of us celebrate tomorrow, Areopagus auditors sneered—and it's often that way among today's academic elite.

We can learn a lot here from the biblical Daniel's ups and downs and ups. In chapter five of his book he predicts the dramatic demise of Belshazzar, and in the very next chapter he's thrown from power into the lion's den. He survives through God's grace and we learn at the end of the chapter that "Daniel prospered during the reign of Darius and the reign of Cyrus the Persian." But we're also told at the beginning of chapter ten that in the third year of Cyrus's reign Daniel was mourning for three weeks, apparently in connection with a political development, until he had "a great vision" of war in the heavens.

Daniel remembered at this point that he was only a small hobbit in a great big universal conflict. We also have to think along those lines, standing for Christ but standing ready to work with others by learning the ABCs of co-belligerency in America:

A: ASSESS accurately both past and present. Western civilization is founded on both Jerusalem and Athens, biblical and classical knowledge, and just as it's not accurate for liberal professors to ignore the Bible, so it's not accurate for conservative Christians to say that non-biblical strains were unimportant in the formation of Western civilization or America itself. Christianity was crucial in the founding of the United States, but some deists and skeptics also were part of the revolutionary coalition.

B: BUILD consensus in our own ranks. The Calvinist concept of "lesser magistrates"—local officials standing up against monarchs— is a mighty one, but "magistrates" is plural, not singular. Individual rebellion can be quirky, so the requirement that many magistrates hang together makes sure that the grievances are great. Our opponents are secular liberals, not other Christian conservatives, and rhetoric that divides us helps our adversaries to conquer. One question to ask before mounting any offensive: is it likely to drive back the left or merely purge our own ranks?

C: CHOOSE battles and tactics carefully. Sometimes we have no choice of battleground. If we are ordered to stop praying to God or to bow to idols, we must stand firm wherever we are, as did Daniel and his friends in ancient Babylon. But when we do have a choice, we need to emphasize life-changing questions such as abortion and marriage. If we lose we lose, but we should try to win, not rush toward martyrdom when other God-honoring options exist. Otherwise, it's not martyrdom: it's suicide.

If we follow those ABCs, we won't adopt the terrible tactic of spam recruitment: making statements that excite one listener but turn off a thousand. Some with a defeatist mentality assume that minds cannot change, so their goal is to propel into action those already in their camp—and to the devil with others. They are like spam e-mailers, not caring how many get irritated as they make a sale. That hurts not only Christian social and political activity but evangelism as well.

If we understand the need to assess, build, and choose, we also won't send eviction notices to those who do not agree with our particular set of tactics. God wanted Gideon's army to be small, but that was based on special revelation. Today, efforts designed to create a tiny hard core by attacking other Christian conservatives who disagree tactically owe more to Lenin than to the Bible. We mustn't forget that the difference between left and right is far greater than differences among Christian conservatives.

Remembering the ABCs gives us our best opportunity, within God's providence, of avoiding the big F of failure. (2004)

Tax and Credit

Impasse.

Democrats want higher taxes on the rich and say GOP stalwarts are "selfish." Republicans oppose tax hikes and say the Dems are big-government empire-builders.

Impasse? Not necessarily. I have a proposal. Stick with me, please, as I set it up.

Many Democrats claim their purpose is not to gain more power by centralizing political and economic authority. They say they want "fairness." They say the rich benefit by working in a mostly-free economy and should "give back" to America some of what they've gained by being Americans. (Actually, many among the rich build and invest in businesses that create jobs and opportunity for the not-rich, but let's not debate this right now.)

Many Republicans don't trust Washington to spend wisely any new tax revenues, but they claim to be at least as public-spirited as their opponents. Evidence backs them up: Arthur Brooks showed in *Who Really Cares?* (Basic, 2006) that conservatives give more to charity than liberals do. (Some of this giving goes to tony private schools and other nonprofits that largely profit the families of the rich, but let's not debate that right now.)

Let's grant each side its self-portrayal: Democrats want to keep the poor from starving, and Republicans want to keep the federal government from becoming fatter. We can break that impasse by using tax-and-credit. Let's give President Obama, his Capitol Hill colleagues, and Warren Buffett the prize they desire: Raise rates on the top one percent. Let's give the top one percent the opportunity to show their public-spiritedness: Provide a 100 percent tax credit on those additional taxes so they can use that money not to grow Washington but to grow opportunities for the poor.

Here's how it works, in a simplified form: Susie with a two million dollar income has her tax bill increase by $56,000, according to the Obama proposal. If she believes with Buffet that the federal government should have more money, she sends it in. Score one for Democrats. But Susie has an option. If she decides to give the $56,000 to religious or secular anti-poverty efforts, or job-creating business incubators, she writes checks to those organizations and attaches their acknowledgment letters to her tax form. She doesn't enable Washington bureaucrats. Score one for Republicans.

My proposal has problems. It won't do as much to trim the deficit as a straight tax increase (combined with much larger spending decreases) would. Raising taxes in a near-recession could be a disincentive to job formation in the private, for-profit sector.

Yet, this approach satisfies both Democratic demands that the top one percent pay more, and Republican desires that no one be forced to send more dollars to wasteful Washington. This approach would create jobs in non-profits that provide effective compassion. A stronger civil society would lead to less government.

Some conservatives will complain that all of Susie's money is hers to use any way she wants—but Christians know that all of us are responsible before God to be stewards, not owners, of the resources He gives us. A tax credit approach helps the poor while maximizing donor choice and minimizing government aggrandizement.

I recognize that this is a bridge too far for non-theistic conservative theoreticians, so for them I'd propose Madisonian realism. Liberals who engage in class warfare have a destructive but potentially winning argument in today's culture. Conservatives need to undercut their appeal.

Even greater opposition is likely to arise from the liberal side. In 1995 I met with six leading Democratic senators who were complaining about prospective GOP cuts in welfare expenditures. I proposed a grand bargain: No cuts, but decentralize welfare. They were unwilling to give up their power. They said no.

We'll probably get a "no" this time as well, but even if my proposal is dead on arrival among liberals it will smoke out those whose real concern is not "fairness" but power.

And what if, miraculously, we get a "yes" from enough people on both sides to have Congress pass a tax-and-credit measure? Civil society, the American way of working together without growing government, gets a big boost. Good poverty-fighting programs, often starved for funds as government grabs more and more, increase their funding base.

Liberty and opportunity increase, rather than decrease.

Impasse? It doesn't have to be that way. (1997)

Patriotism Amid Shame

Two hundred and thirty years ago this week the American Revolution began, so Monday is Patriots' Day in Massachusetts and Maine—but after the Terri Schiavo tragedy many Christians are not thinking particularly patriotic thoughts. "I'm so ashamed of our country," one reader wrote.

We should be ashamed. We should pray and work hard, hoping that Terri Schaivo's death is not in vain. But we shouldn't be surprised when bad things happen, and we shouldn't think of the United States as a holy land suddenly blemished. America is not the new Israel and it never was.

This country is an arena in which Christians can stand for Christ while others stand for ungodly philosophies. Some of those philosophies have gained greater traction recently, but they've been here in some form since colonial days, and it's not the Christian task to ban them in the way that ancient Israel (according to chapter 18 of Deuteronomy) was to banish fortune-tellers, omen-interpreters, and sorcerers.

Lest we feel totally downcast and God-abandoned, we should remember that the Old Testament is highly location-specific. It was so important to keep the Holy Land holy that the policy was zero tolerance: No abominations in Israel. Nothing. Nada. Penalties for disobedience in the land were severe, and God also established many specific practices for that land: familial property was not to be sold, cities of refuge were to be established, and so forth.

What God presented, in short, was an opportunity for Israelites to set up a new version of one kind of Eden: not the Eden at the beginning of Genesis (because sin would still burden man, the earth would still yield its produce reluctantly, and earthly life would still end in death) but a semi-Eden, not quite a garden but certainly a land flowing in milk and honey.

The semi-Eden carried with it God's semi-presence: God did not walk with Israelites but He did facilitate prophecy and give specific advice via the casting of lots and the mysterious Urim and Thummim (which do not reappear after the Babylonian captivity). God chose a particular nation to live in His semi-Eden, provided commandments so they knew what to do day by day, inspired a history so they knew where they came from, and promised them that if they obeyed all would go well.

This holy land, this semi-Eden, "a green olive tree, beautiful with good fruit (Jeremiah 11:16), was supposed to be spotless, a serious equivalent of Disneyland in which not a single candy wrapper is to stay on the ground for more than a few minutes. The prophets were indignant when, as God had Jeremiah proclaim, "you defiled my land and made my heritage an abomination." (That defilement, of course, showed the desperate need of man for Christ; living in the best possible environment made little difference.)

But Jeremiah has a very different tone when he speaks to Israelites who live not only outside the semi-Eden but in the anti-Eden, Babylon: Israelites there were to "build houses and live in them; plant gardens and eat their produce. . . . Seek the welfare of the city where I have sent you into exile, and pray to the LORD on its behalf, because in its welfare you will find your welfare" (Jeremiah 29:4–7).

Other parts of the Old Testament also indicate that Israelites outside the borders of Israel had a different agenda than those inside. The book of Daniel shows how Daniel had to hang out with enchanters, sorcerers, and the other wise men of Babylon, the very sorts of people banned in Israel. The books of Esther and Nehemiah show how God's people in Persia lived amid evil yet were the most patriotic of subjects: Cupbearer Nehemiah was the last defense against attempts to poison the king. Mordecai in the book of Esther broke up an assassination plot. When Esther and her uncle Mordecai later had an opportunity to have the king promulgate legislation, they requested that the Jews of Persia have the right to fight back militarily against their persecutors.

Importantly, none of the Israelites' public acceptance of differences indicated a failure to keep God's commands in their own households and gatherings—but some other things were beyond their control. They did the best they could, with God's grace, and when they lost they prepared for the next time biblical and pagan worldviews would come into conflict. We can patriotically do the same. (2006)

New Year's Resolutions

First question in the famous Westminster Shorter Catechism: "What is the chief end of man?" Answer: "to glorify God and enjoy Him forever."

Over the past decade many evangelicals have sounded alarms about low church involvement among millennials (commonly defined as those born from 1982 through 2000). Others say the situation isn't so dire: With young people marrying and having children later, re-attaching to churches will also come later. Who's right? One thing to keep in mind: The good old days weren't always good. Leigh Eric Schmidt's *Village Atheists* (Princeton, 2016), a history of popular atheism and agnosticism in America, describes how Ernestine Rose attracted 2,000 residents of Bangor, Maine, to an 1855 speech attacking belief in God, and atheist Robert Ingersoll sold out his coast-to-coach lecture tours from the 1870s through the 1890s.

We somehow think colleges have suddenly gone down the drain theologically, but the American Association for the Advancement of Atheism had chapters on twenty college campuses in the 1920s. The *New York Times* reported a Yale student group's "platform that the old religion is bunk, that God is a figment of the diseased mind, and Heaven a luscious frankfurter hold out on the end of a stick to keep the anthropoid rabble working like the trained dog in a circus."

Public opinion surveys do not clearly show us how many agnostic-sounding millennials have thought things through and how many are reacting to what they see as church hypocrisy or over-politicization. It's worth asking: What difference would it make if more evangelicals, before taking positions on particular issues, believed our primary task is to glorify God—and then to enjoy seeing the spectacular things He does?

This brings me to a pre-election dinner I had with three Austin millennial evangelicals who volunteered long hours to make a statement they thought would glorify God. Regardless of your politics, I hope you'll appreciate their concern for Christian witness in our country.

The three—Paul Hastings, 26, Alex Lerma, 24, and Nathan Webster, 31—were all home-schooled. They are now business consultants and video/film makers. Four weeks before election day they used vacation days from work and gathered a team of volunteer animators, logo designers, web developers, and attorneys. Their goal: to create a website, Truth Trumps Fear, and a video they shot in Alex's brother's living room.

Their key theological point: "We are called to holiness. God and God alone will save our country. We should never cast a vote out of fear unless it is the fear of God." Two weeks before election day the video went live, then viral on Facebook, reaching 1.2 million people in all.

"Viral" these days does not mean just happening, with no marketing work involved. The three musketeers emailed friends who emailed their friends. Once the number of page views started growing, they emailed influential conservatives. They also understood how Facebook algorithms work—posts that users share or comment about get improved placement.

All three said their homeschool backgrounds helped: They had learned how to teach themselves, say what they think is right, and not fear how others react. Again, their political judgment may have been right, or wrong, but I'm impressed that they—after growing up amid the biggest entertainment-industrial complex in history, and its corrosive irony and sarcasm—still wanted to rely on God.

Their attitude is very different from that of the millennials who after the election went on rampages or fell into crying sessions. Hastings, post-election, told me he and his associates know that "No matter what may come, God is still in control and we are His people. If we are His people, let us live like we are." They are praying for President-elect Trump, as should all of us.

In late December many people make new year's resolutions, but few keep them more than a week. Chapter 5 of Ecclesiastes says, "Be not rash with your mouth, nor let your heart be hasty to utter a word before God, for God is in heaven and you are on earth. Therefore let your words be few" (v. 2).

For Christians, only one resolution is crucial: to desire, through God's grace, to glorify Him and enjoy Him forever. That means being a branch, as Christ says in John 15:5: "I am the vine; you are the branches . . . for apart from me you can do nothing." (2016)

Final Note

Communion with St. Paul

"This is Christ's body, broken for you. This is Christ's blood, shed for you." As we give out bread and wine during the Lord's Supper, the actor is Jesus, the beneficiary is personal: you.

Ads last month on Ethiopian radio spoke of a "cleft clinic," a Project CURE program for children and adults with holes in their faces and their throats. I watched one afternoon last month as twenty patients, usually brought by their parents, came to Paul Lim, an American plastic surgeon who recently sacrificed security and a colossal income to move with his young family to Addis Ababa, the east African country's capital.

God's mercy is evident in both the Lord's Supper and the fact that most of us are born with faces with the right number of holes. At six-to-eight weeks of gestation our faces usually fuse. For some reason, in some children, the parts don't fuse. They have extra holes between their noses and their lips. They need additional grace.

"We'll make his nose better," Lim (through a translator) told one mother holding her baby. "We'll make his lip better. Jesus brought us, brought me, here for him." The mom left wordlessly.

A twenty-three-year-old who could be very pretty except for her malformation came in, looking ready to cry. She had unskilled surgery as a child and is now a teacher, with students who sometimes hoot at her. Lim: "We'll make your nose better. Jesus brought me here for you." She walked out, dazed: Will this miracle come to pass?

A teenaged mom walked in holding a one-month-old with a completely cleft lip. She sat, gazed at her baby, and smiled—no, glowed: She's in love with her baby. The father, a few years older, wearing a Michael Jordan 23 shirt, was unsmiling. When Lim said, "We will fix his lip," the mom beamed even more broadly, but the father remained stern.

Then Lim said, "Jesus brought me, brought us, here for him." The man suddenly smiled, as if just getting it, and enthusiastically shook the doctor's hand.

A thirteen-year-old girl slipped in, holding up her scarf to cover her mouth. She uncovered her mouth only when seated before Lim—and her reason for hiding behind her scarf was immediately obvious. Lim maintained his composure, examined her, and said to the translator, "Tell her that she will need more than one operation. We will do everything we can to help. Jesus brought us here, brought us all here, for her."

The girl again covered her mouth as she went out. Lim mentioned to me, "That's the first time I've seen this in person. We don't have this in the US—I only saw pictures before."

A twelve-year-old came in with his mouth frozen in a grimace. Malnourishment had provided the base for an infection when he was five. Now he is missing a lot of tissue, skin, and part of his mouth. He had wanted to commit suicide, but Lim said, "We can help you. Jesus brought me, brought us here, for you." The grimace did not, could not (for now) change—but it will.

A father arrived from fifty miles away with his baby, who was dehydrated and shaking. The baby will get immediate help, and the operation will come later. Lim: "By God's grace we have an expert here on feeding children with cleft lip. Jesus brought us here for your son. That's why we are here."

Chapter 22 of Luke's gospel: At the first Communion, on Passover, Jesus "took bread, and when he had given thanks, he broke it and gave it to them, saying, 'This is my body, which is given for you.'"

Communion with St. Paul Lim in Addis Ababa: To a seven-year-old in a Yao 11 NBA shirt, "We will take care of this. Jesus brought me here for you."

Two millennia ago Israelites asked Jesus why a man was born blind. He responded: "that the works of God might be displayed in him." Why are some born with a cleft palate? The answer could be similar: So that God will be glorified through the works of those He calls to help. (2008)

Other Books by Marvin Olasky

On American History

- *The American Leadership Tradition: Moral Vision from Washington to Clinton*
- *Fighting for Liberty and Virtue: Political and Cultural Wars in Eighteenth-Century America*
- *The Politics of Disaster: Katrina, Big Government, and a New Strategy for Future Crises*
- *Philanthropically Correct: The Story of the Council on Foundations*
- *Abortion Rites: A Social History of Abortion in America*
- *Corporate Public Relations: A New Historical Perspective*

On Fighting Poverty

- *Compassionate Conservatism: What it is, What it Does, and How it Can Transform America*
- *Renewing American Compassion*
- *The Tragedy of American Compassion*
- *Patterns of Corporate Philanthropy: Funding False Compassion*
- *More Than Kindness: A Compassionate Approach to Crisis Childbearing* (with Susan Olasky)

On Religion

- *The Religions Next Door: What We Need to Know about Judaism, Hinduism, Buddhism and Islam—and What Reporters are Missing*
- *Unmerited Mercy*

- *Standing for Christ in a Modern Babylon*
- *Turning Point: A Christian Worldview Declaration* (with Herbert Schlossberg)

On Journalism

- *Telling the Truth: How to Revitalize Christian Journalism*
- *Central Ideas in the Development of American Journalism: A Narrative History*
- *The Press and Abortion, 1838–1988*
- *Prodigal Press: The Anti-Christian Bias of the American News Media*
- *Whirled Views: Tracking Today's Cultural Storms* (with Joel Belz)

Fiction

- *Scimitar's Edge*
- *2048: A Story of America's Future*
- *Echoes of Eden*